Walt Disney's Donald Duck
The Abominator

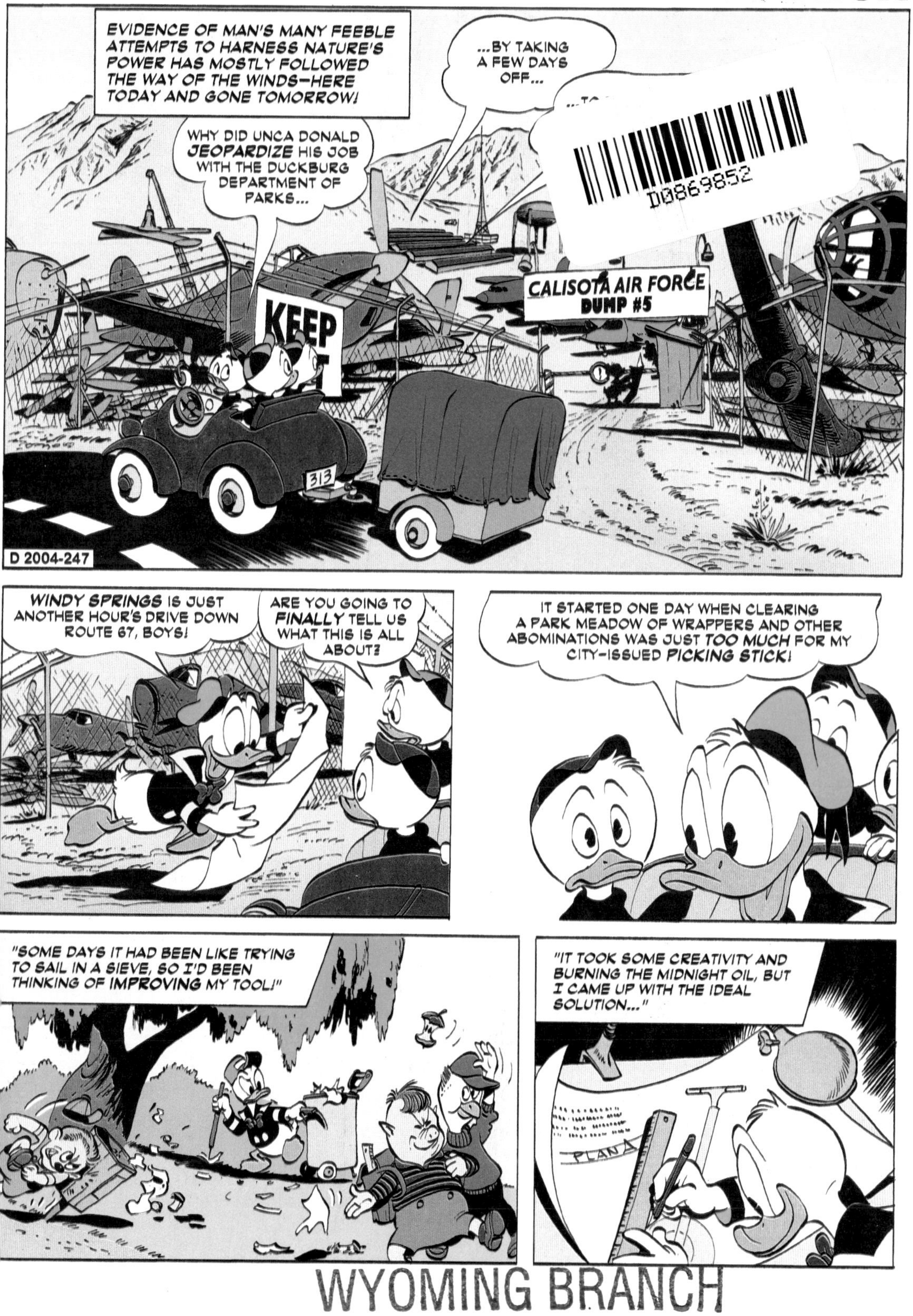
EVIDENCE OF MAN'S MANY FEEBLE ATTEMPTS TO HARNESS NATURE'S POWER HAS MOSTLY FOLLOWED THE WAY OF THE WINDS—HERE TODAY AND GONE TOMORROW!
WHY DID UNCA DONALD JEOPARDIZE HIS JOB WITH THE DUCKBURG DEPARTMENT OF PARKS...
...BY TAKING A FEW DAYS OFF...
KEEP
CALISOTA AIR FORCE DUMP #5
313
D 2004-247
WINDY SPRINGS IS JUST ANOTHER HOUR'S DRIVE DOWN ROUTE 67, BOYS!
ARE YOU GOING TO FINALLY TELL US WHAT THIS IS ALL ABOUT?
IT STARTED ONE DAY WHEN CLEARING A PARK MEADOW OF WRAPPERS AND OTHER ABOMINATIONS WAS JUST TOO MUCH FOR MY CITY-ISSUED PICKING STICK!
"SOME DAYS IT HAD BEEN LIKE TRYING TO SAIL IN A SIEVE, SO I'D BEEN THINKING OF IMPROVING MY TOOL!"
"IT TOOK SOME CREATIVITY AND BURNING THE MIDNIGHT OIL, BUT I CAME UP WITH THE IDEAL SOLUTION..."
PLAN A

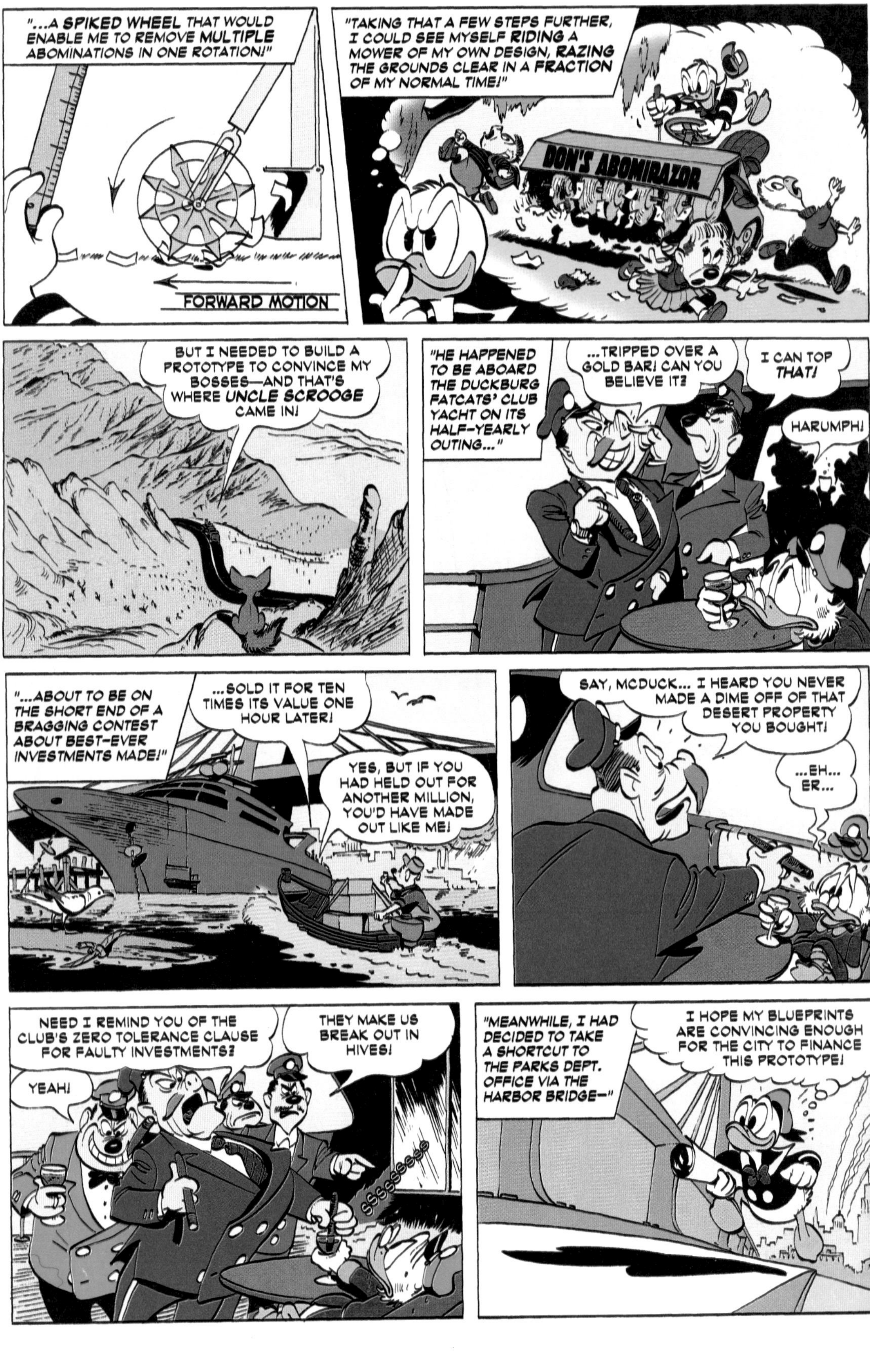
"...A SPIKED WHEEL THAT WOULD ENABLE ME TO REMOVE MULTIPLE ABOMINATIONS IN ONE ROTATION!"
FORWARD MOTION
"TAKING THAT A FEW STEPS FURTHER, I COULD SEE MYSELF RIDING A MOWER OF MY OWN DESIGN, RAZING THE GROUNDS CLEAR IN A FRACTION OF MY NORMAL TIME!"
DON'S ABOMIRAZOR
BUT I NEEDED TO BUILD A PROTOTYPE TO CONVINCE MY BOSSES—AND THAT'S WHERE UNCLE SCROOGE CAME IN!
"HE HAPPENED TO BE ABOARD THE DUCKBURG FATCATS' CLUB YACHT ON ITS HALF-YEARLY OUTING..."
...TRIPPED OVER A GOLD BAR! CAN YOU BELIEVE IT?
I CAN TOP THAT!
HARUMPH!
"...ABOUT TO BE ON THE SHORT END OF A BRAGGING CONTEST ABOUT BEST-EVER INVESTMENTS MADE!"
...SOLD IT FOR TEN TIMES ITS VALUE ONE HOUR LATER!
YES, BUT IF YOU HAD HELD OUT FOR ANOTHER MILLION, YOU'D HAVE MADE OUT LIKE ME!
SAY, MCDUCK... I HEARD YOU NEVER MADE A DIME OFF OF THAT DESERT PROPERTY YOU BOUGHT!
...EH... ER...
NEED I REMIND YOU OF THE CLUB'S ZERO TOLERANCE CLAUSE FOR FAULTY INVESTMENTS?
THEY MAKE US BREAK OUT IN HIVES!
YEAH!
SSSSSSSSS
"MEANWHILE, I HAD DECIDED TO TAKE A SHORTCUT TO THE PARKS DEPT. OFFICE VIA THE HARBOR BRIDGE—"
I HOPE MY BLUEPRINTS ARE CONVINCING ENOUGH FOR THE CITY TO FINANCE THIS PROTOTYPE!

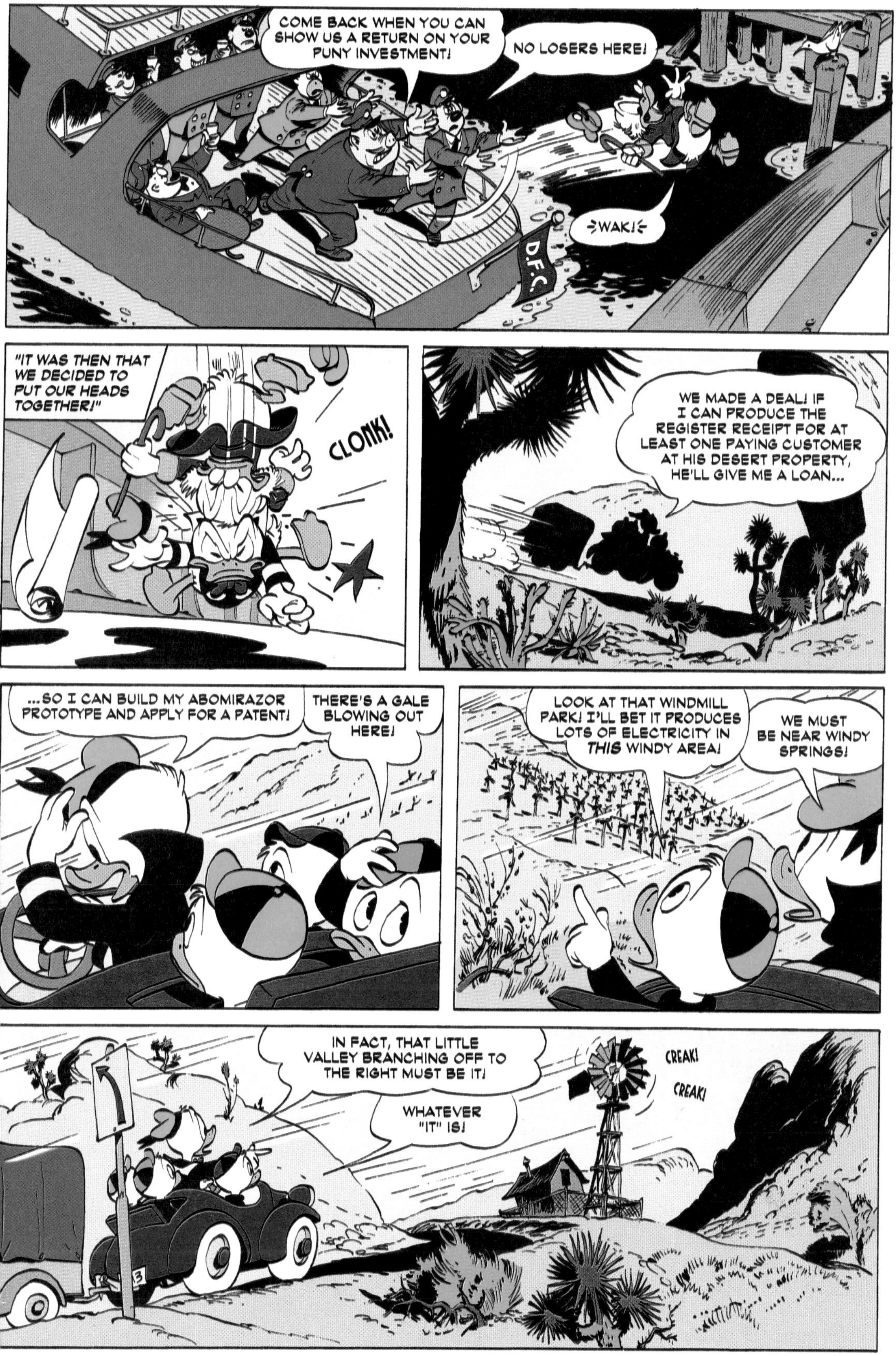
COME BACK WHEN YOU CAN SHOW US A RETURN ON YOUR PUNY INVESTMENT!
NO LOSERS HERE!
WAK!
"IT WAS THEN THAT WE DECIDED TO PUT OUR HEADS TOGETHER!"
CLONK!
D.F.C.
WE MADE A DEAL! IF I CAN PRODUCE THE REGISTER RECEIPT FOR AT LEAST ONE PAYING CUSTOMER AT HIS DESERT PROPERTY, HE'LL GIVE ME A LOAN...
...SO I CAN BUILD MY ABOMIRAZOR PROTOTYPE AND APPLY FOR A PATENT!
THERE'S A GALE BLOWING OUT HERE!
LOOK AT THAT WINDMILL PARK! I'LL BET IT PRODUCES LOTS OF ELECTRICITY IN *THIS* WINDY AREA!
WE MUST BE NEAR WINDY SPRINGS!
IN FACT, THAT LITTLE VALLEY BRANCHING OFF TO THE RIGHT MUST BE IT!
WHATEVER "IT" IS!
CREAK!
CREAK!

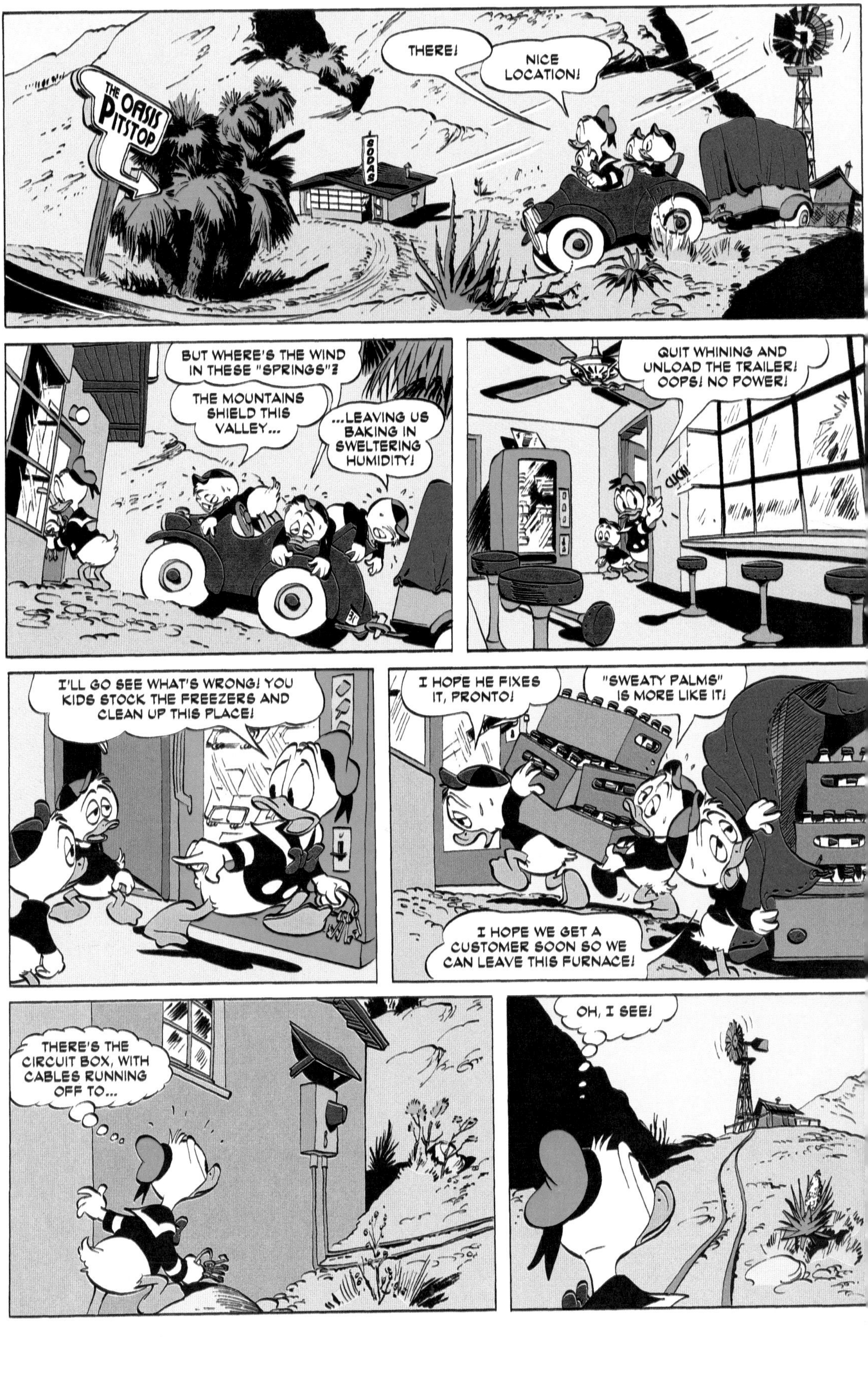
THE OASIS PITSTOP
SODAS
THERE!
NICE LOCATION!
BUT WHERE'S THE WIND IN THESE "SPRINGS"?
THE MOUNTAINS SHIELD THIS VALLEY...
...LEAVING US BAKING IN SWELTERING HUMIDITY!
QUIT WHINING AND UNLOAD THE TRAILER! OOPS! NO POWER!
CLICK!
I'LL GO SEE WHAT'S WRONG! YOU KIDS STOCK THE FREEZERS AND CLEAN UP THIS PLACE!
I HOPE HE FIXES IT, PRONTO!
"SWEATY PALMS" IS MORE LIKE IT!
I HOPE WE GET A CUSTOMER SOON SO WE CAN LEAVE THIS FURNACE!
THERE'S THE CIRCUIT BOX, WITH CABLES RUNNING OFF TO...
OH, I SEE!

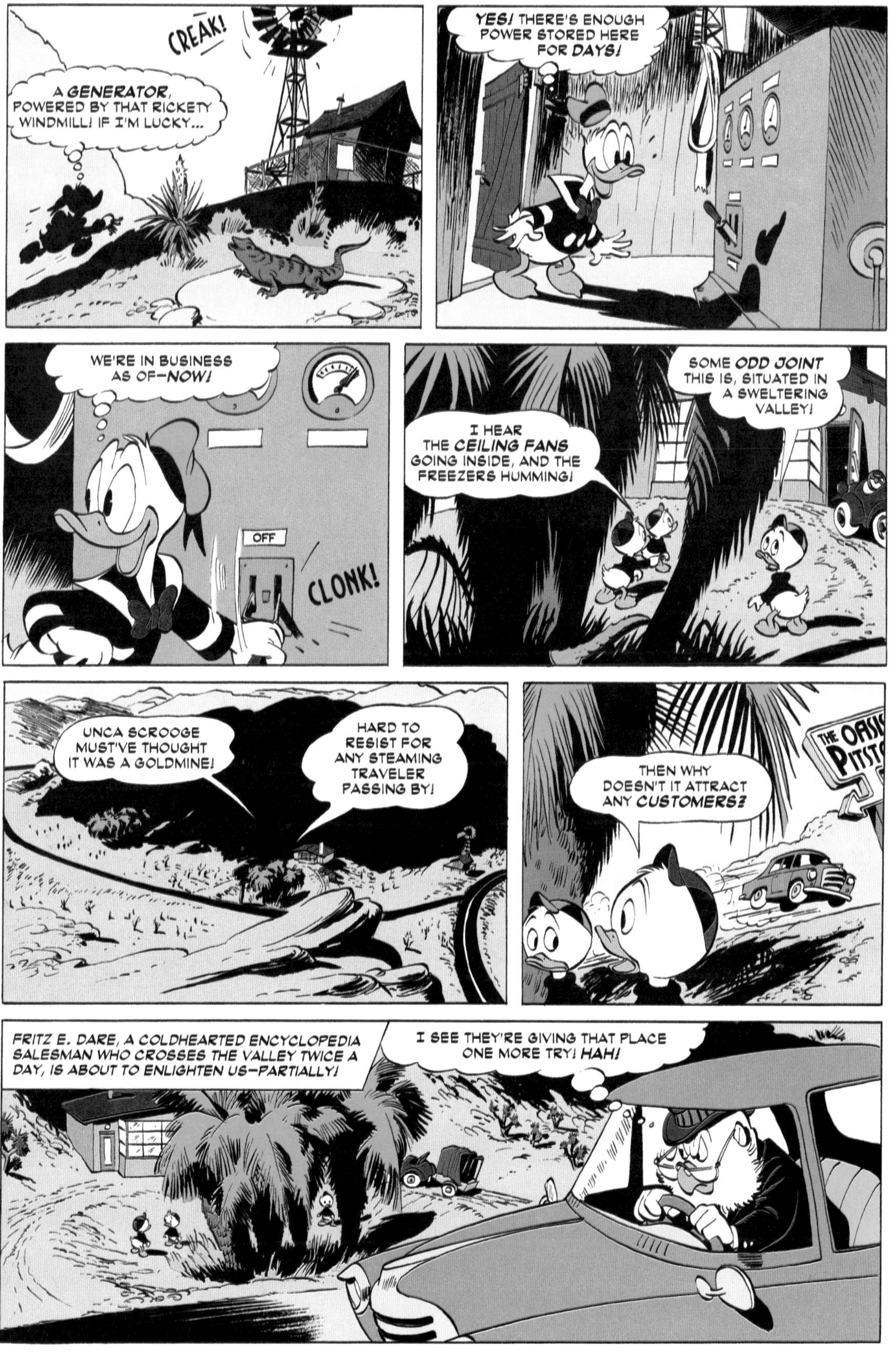
A GENERATOR, POWERED BY THAT RICKETY WINDMILL! IF I'M LUCKY...
CREAK!
YES! THERE'S ENOUGH POWER STORED HERE FOR DAYS!
WE'RE IN BUSINESS AS OF—NOW!
OFF
CLONK!
SOME ODD JOINT THIS IS, SITUATED IN A SWELTERING VALLEY!
I HEAR THE CEILING FANS GOING INSIDE, AND THE FREEZERS HUMMING!
UNCA SCROOGE MUST'VE THOUGHT IT WAS A GOLDMINE!
HARD TO RESIST FOR ANY STEAMING TRAVELER PASSING BY!
THEN WHY DOESN'T IT ATTRACT ANY CUSTOMERS?
FRITZ E. DARE, A COLDHEARTED ENCYCLOPEDIA SALESMAN WHO CROSSES THE VALLEY TWICE A DAY, IS ABOUT TO ENLIGHTEN US—PARTIALLY!
I SEE THEY'RE GIVING THAT PLACE ONE MORE TRY! HAH!

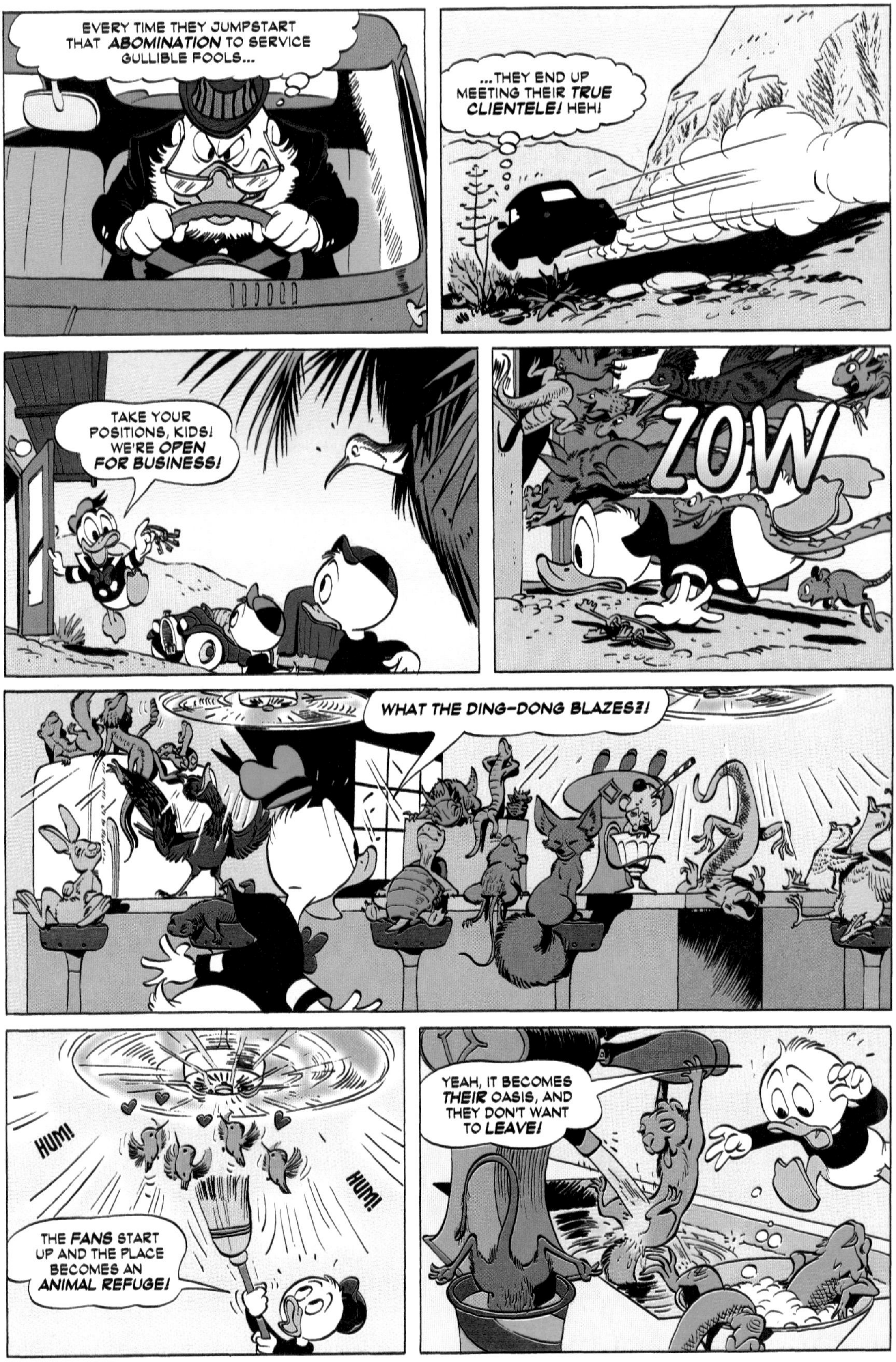
EVERY TIME THEY JUMPSTART THAT ABOMINATION TO SERVICE GULLIBLE FOOLS...
...THEY END UP MEETING THEIR TRUE CLIENTELE! HEH!
TAKE YOUR POSITIONS, KIDS! WE'RE OPEN FOR BUSINESS!
ZOW
WHAT THE DING-DONG BLAZES?!
HUM!
HUM!
THE FANS START UP AND THE PLACE BECOMES AN ANIMAL REFUGE!
YEAH, IT BECOMES THEIR OASIS, AND THEY DON'T WANT TO LEAVE!

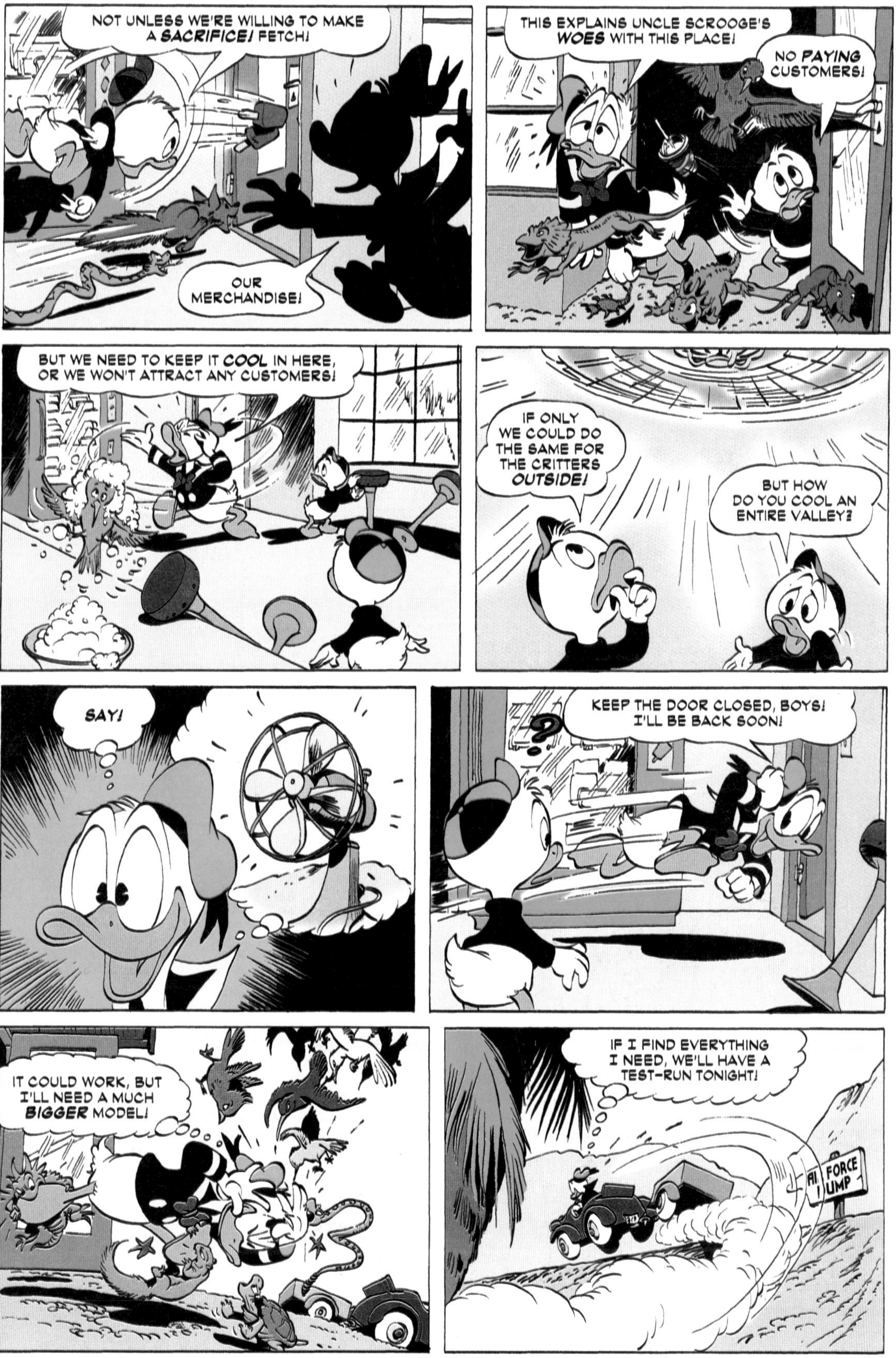
NOT UNLESS WE'RE WILLING TO MAKE A SACRIFICE! FETCH!
OUR MERCHANDISE!
THIS EXPLAINS UNCLE SCROOGE'S WOES WITH THIS PLACE!
NO PAYING CUSTOMERS!
BUT WE NEED TO KEEP IT COOL IN HERE, OR WE WON'T ATTRACT ANY CUSTOMERS!
IF ONLY WE COULD DO THE SAME FOR THE CRITTERS OUTSIDE!
BUT HOW DO YOU COOL AN ENTIRE VALLEY?
SAY!
KEEP THE DOOR CLOSED, BOYS! I'LL BE BACK SOON!
IT COULD WORK, BUT I'LL NEED A MUCH BIGGER MODEL!
IF I FIND EVERYTHING I NEED, WE'LL HAVE A TEST-RUN TONIGHT!
AI FORCE UMP

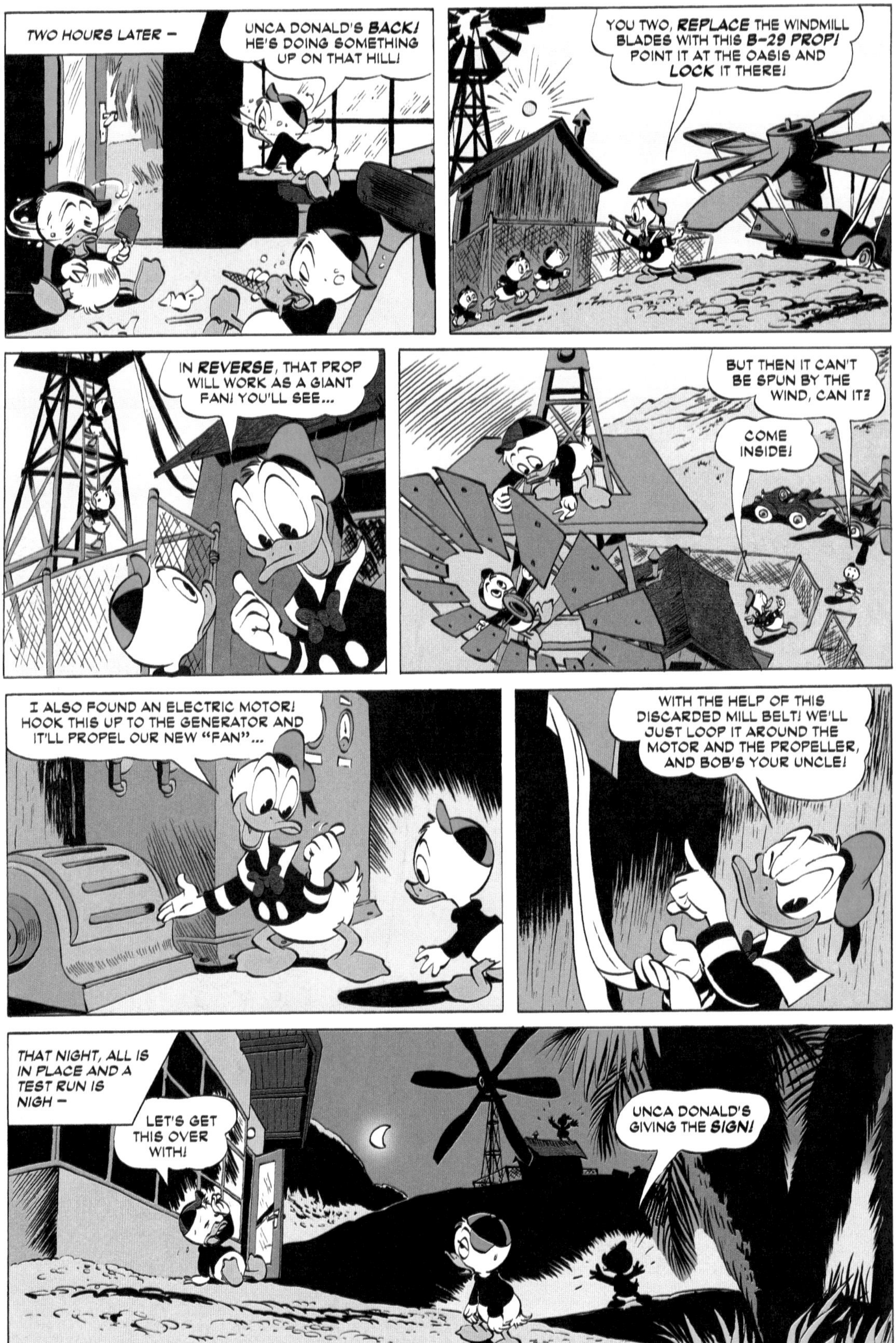
TWO HOURS LATER —
UNCA DONALD'S BACK! HE'S DOING SOMETHING UP ON THAT HILL!
YOU TWO, REPLACE THE WINDMILL BLADES WITH THIS B-29 PROP! POINT IT AT THE OASIS AND LOCK IT THERE!
IN REVERSE, THAT PROP WILL WORK AS A GIANT FAN! YOU'LL SEE...
BUT THEN IT CAN'T BE SPUN BY THE WIND, CAN IT?
COME INSIDE!
I ALSO FOUND AN ELECTRIC MOTOR! HOOK THIS UP TO THE GENERATOR AND IT'LL PROPEL OUR NEW "FAN"...
WITH THE HELP OF THIS DISCARDED MILL BELT! WE'LL JUST LOOP IT AROUND THE MOTOR AND THE PROPELLER, AND BOB'S YOUR UNCLE!
THAT NIGHT, ALL IS IN PLACE AND A TEST RUN IS NIGH —
LET'S GET THIS OVER WITH!
UNCA DONALD'S GIVING THE SIGN!

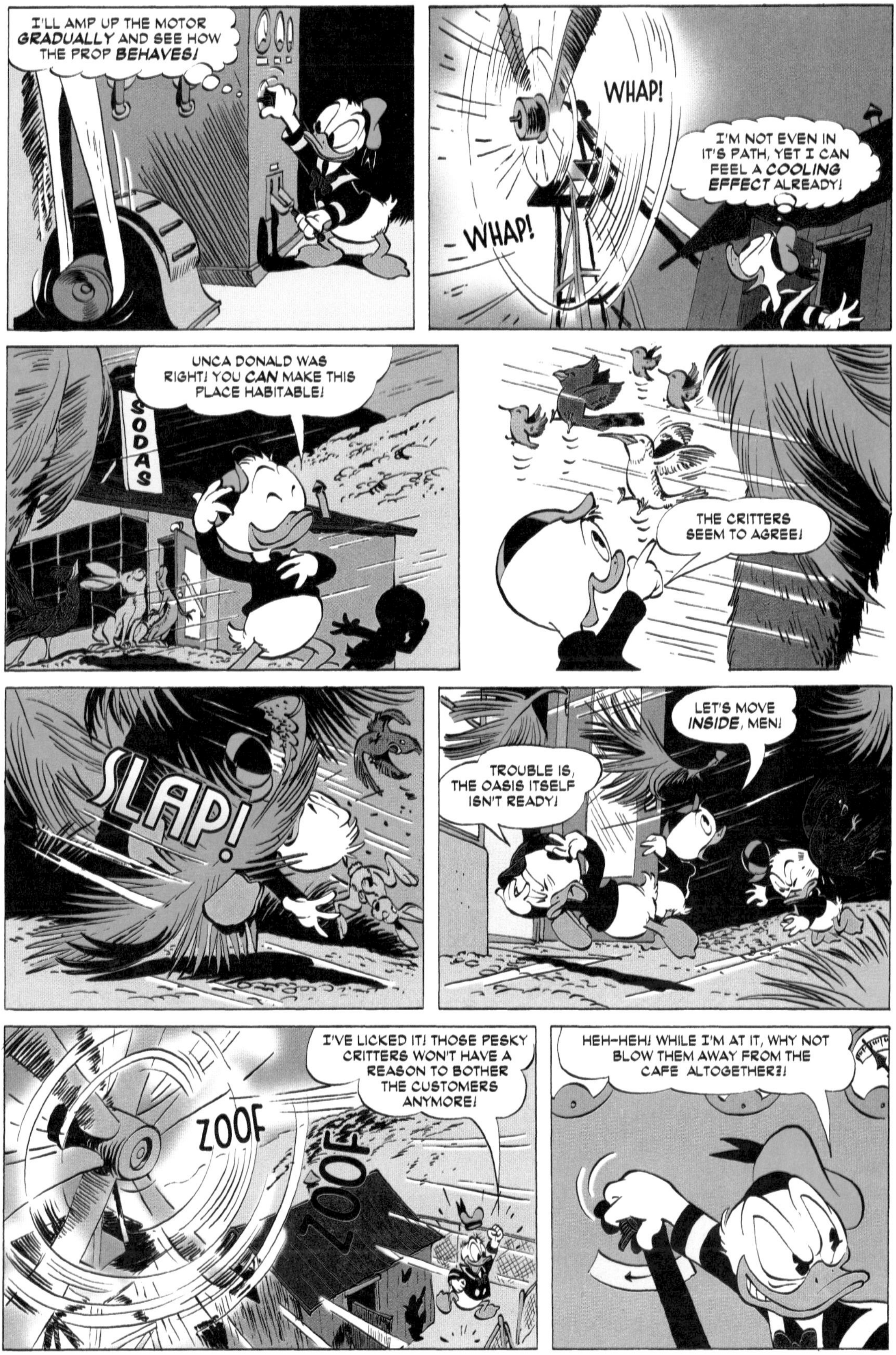

I'LL AMP UP THE MOTOR GRADUALLY AND SEE HOW THE PROP BEHAVES!
WHAP!
I'M NOT EVEN IN IT'S PATH, YET I CAN FEEL A COOLING EFFECT ALREADY!
WHAP!
UNCA DONALD WAS RIGHT! YOU CAN MAKE THIS PLACE HABITABLE!
SODAS
THE CRITTERS SEEM TO AGREE!
SLAP!
LET'S MOVE INSIDE, MEN!
TROUBLE IS, THE OASIS ITSELF ISN'T READY!
I'VE LICKED IT! THOSE PESKY CRITTERS WON'T HAVE A REASON TO BOTHER THE CUSTOMERS ANYMORE!
ZOOF
ZOOF
HEH-HEH! WHILE I'M AT IT, WHY NOT BLOW THEM AWAY FROM THE CAFE ALTOGETHER?!

WHAT'S UNCA DONALD UP TO NOW? HE'S *DESTROYING* THE OASIS!

SLAM!

WHOOSH

WOO-HOO! THIS EXCEEDS MY WILDEST EXPECTATIONS!

CREAK!

?

STOP, UNCA DONALD! *STOP!*

HE CAN'T *HEAR* US FROM HERE!

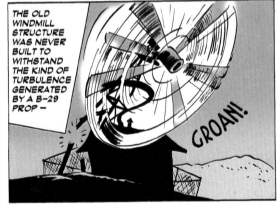

THE OLD WINDMILL STRUCTURE WAS NEVER BUILT TO WITHSTAND THE KIND OF TURBULENCE GENERATED BY A B-29 PROP –

GROAN!

AS THE TOWER TOPPLES OVER, THE PROP'S BLADES BITE INTO THE DESERT –

THE PROP IS WHEELING *STRAIGHT AT US!*

AND THE SAND IT KICKED UP IS *BLOCKING* THE DOOR!

WE CAN'T GET OUT!

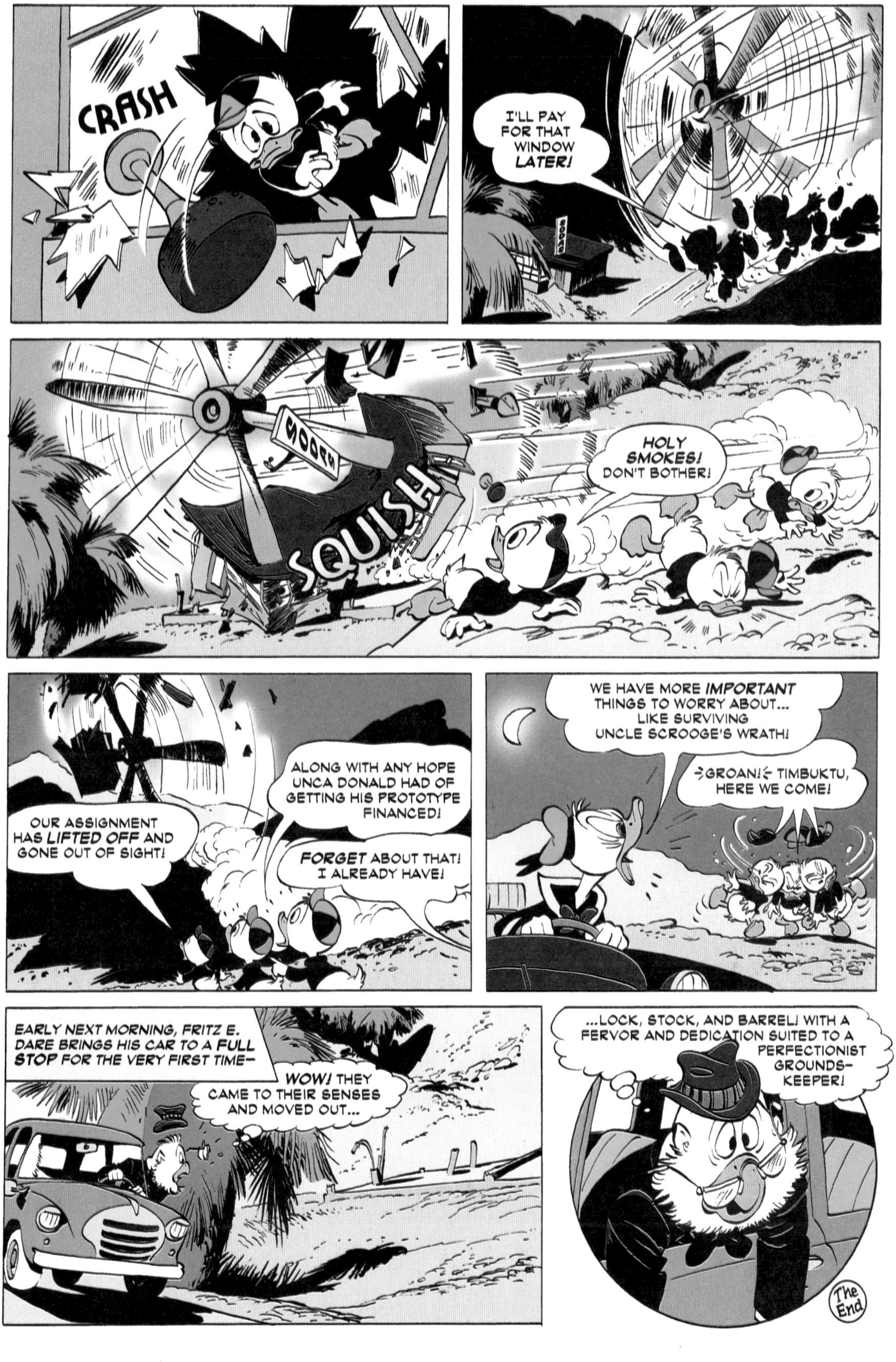
CRASH
I'LL PAY FOR THAT WINDOW LATER!
SODAS
SODAS
SQUISH
HOLY SMOKES! DON'T BOTHER!
OUR ASSIGNMENT HAS LIFTED OFF AND GONE OUT OF SIGHT!
ALONG WITH ANY HOPE UNCA DONALD HAD OF GETTING HIS PROTOTYPE FINANCED!
FORGET ABOUT THAT! I ALREADY HAVE!
WE HAVE MORE IMPORTANT THINGS TO WORRY ABOUT... LIKE SURVIVING UNCLE SCROOGE'S WRATH!
GROAN! TIMBUKTU, HERE WE COME!
EARLY NEXT MORNING, FRITZ E. DARE BRINGS HIS CAR TO A FULL STOP FOR THE VERY FIRST TIME—
WOW! THEY CAME TO THEIR SENSES AND MOVED OUT...
...LOCK, STOCK, AND BARREL! WITH A FERVOR AND DEDICATION SUITED TO A PERFECTIONIST GROUNDS-KEEPER!
The End

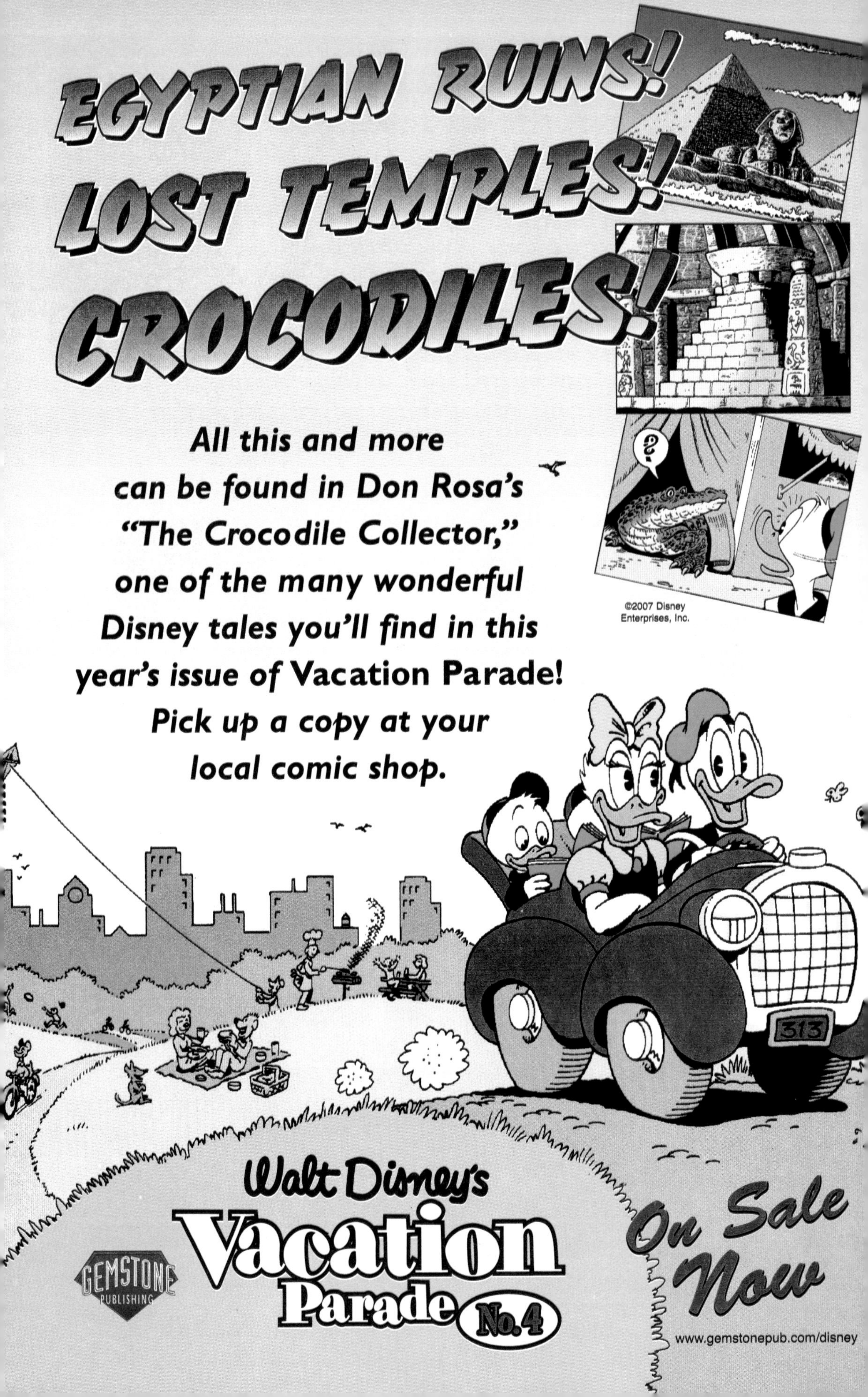
EGYPTIAN RUINS!
LOST TEMPLES!
CROCODILES!
?
All this and more can be found in Don Rosa's "The Crocodile Collector," one of the many wonderful Disney tales you'll find in this year's issue of Vacation Parade! Pick up a copy at your local comic shop.
©2007 Disney Enterprises, Inc.
313
Walt Disney's
Vacation Parade No.4
GEMSTONE PUBLISHING
On Sale Now
www.gemstonepub.com/disney

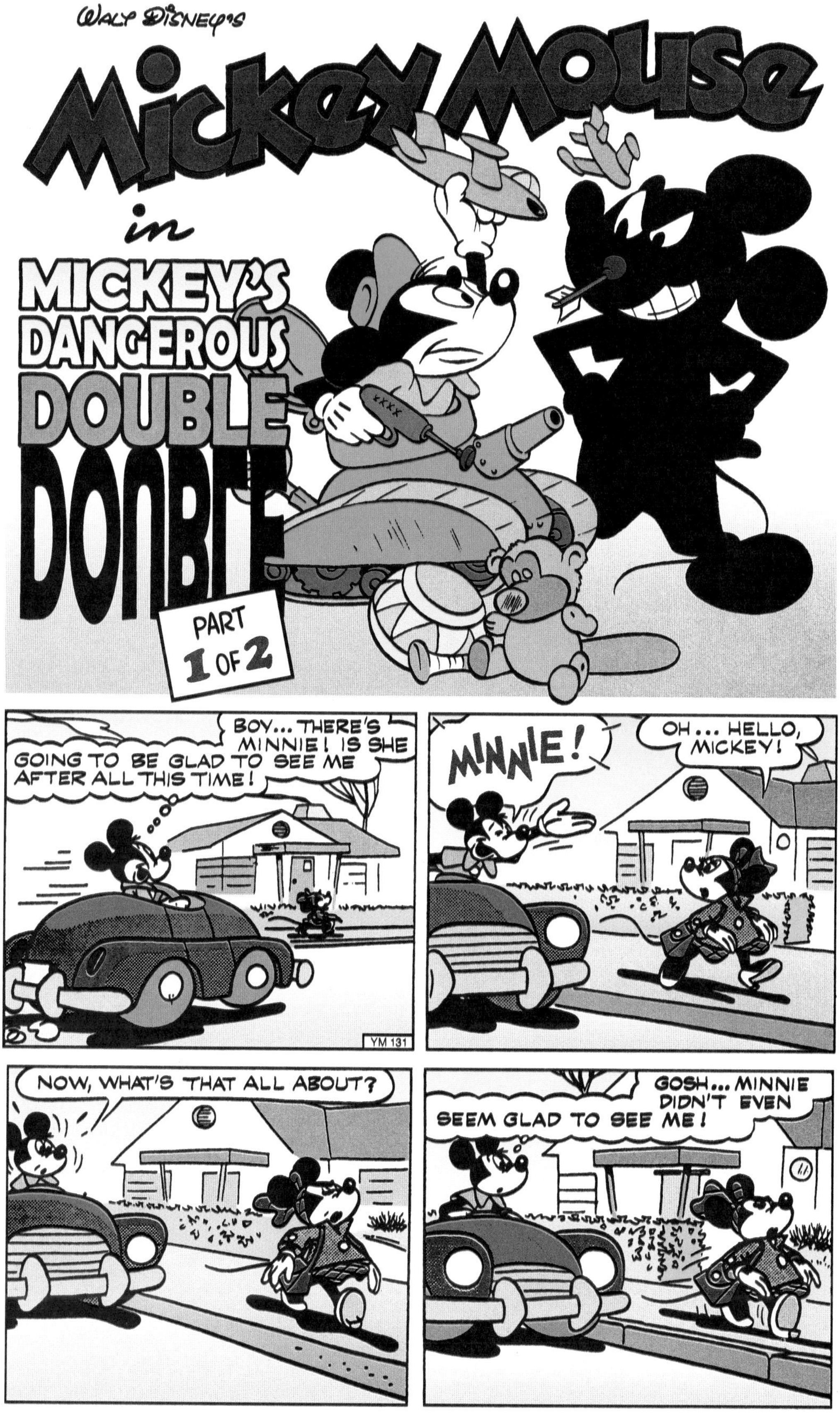

Walt Disney's
Mickey Mouse
in
MICKEY'S DANGEROUS DOUBLE
PART 1 OF 2
BOY... THERE'S MINNIE! IS SHE GOING TO BE GLAD TO SEE ME AFTER ALL THIS TIME!
YM 131
MINNIE!
OH... HELLO, MICKEY!
NOW, WHAT'S THAT ALL ABOUT?
GOSH... MINNIE DIDN'T EVEN SEEM GLAD TO SEE ME!

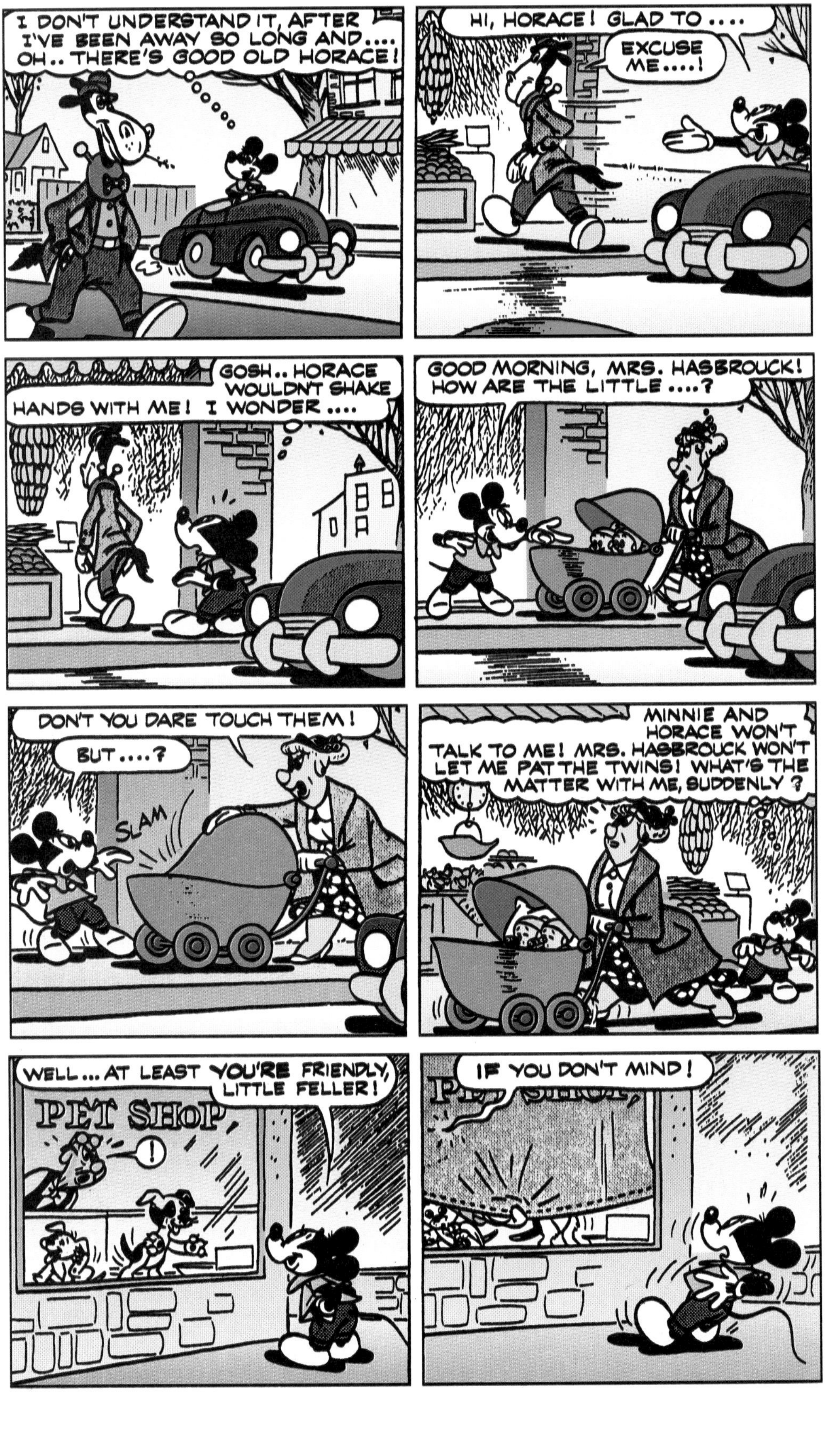
I DON'T UNDERSTAND IT, AFTER I'VE BEEN AWAY SO LONG AND.... OH.. THERE'S GOOD OLD HORACE!
HI, HORACE! GLAD TO ....
EXCUSE ME....!
GOSH.. HORACE WOULDN'T SHAKE HANDS WITH ME! I WONDER ....
GOOD MORNING, MRS. HASBROUCK! HOW ARE THE LITTLE ....?
DON'T YOU DARE TOUCH THEM!
BUT....?
SLAM
MINNIE AND HORACE WON'T TALK TO ME! MRS. HASBROUCK WON'T LET ME PAT THE TWINS! WHAT'S THE MATTER WITH ME, SUDDENLY?
WELL... AT LEAST YOU'RE FRIENDLY, LITTLE FELLER!
PET SHOP
!
IF YOU DON'T MIND!

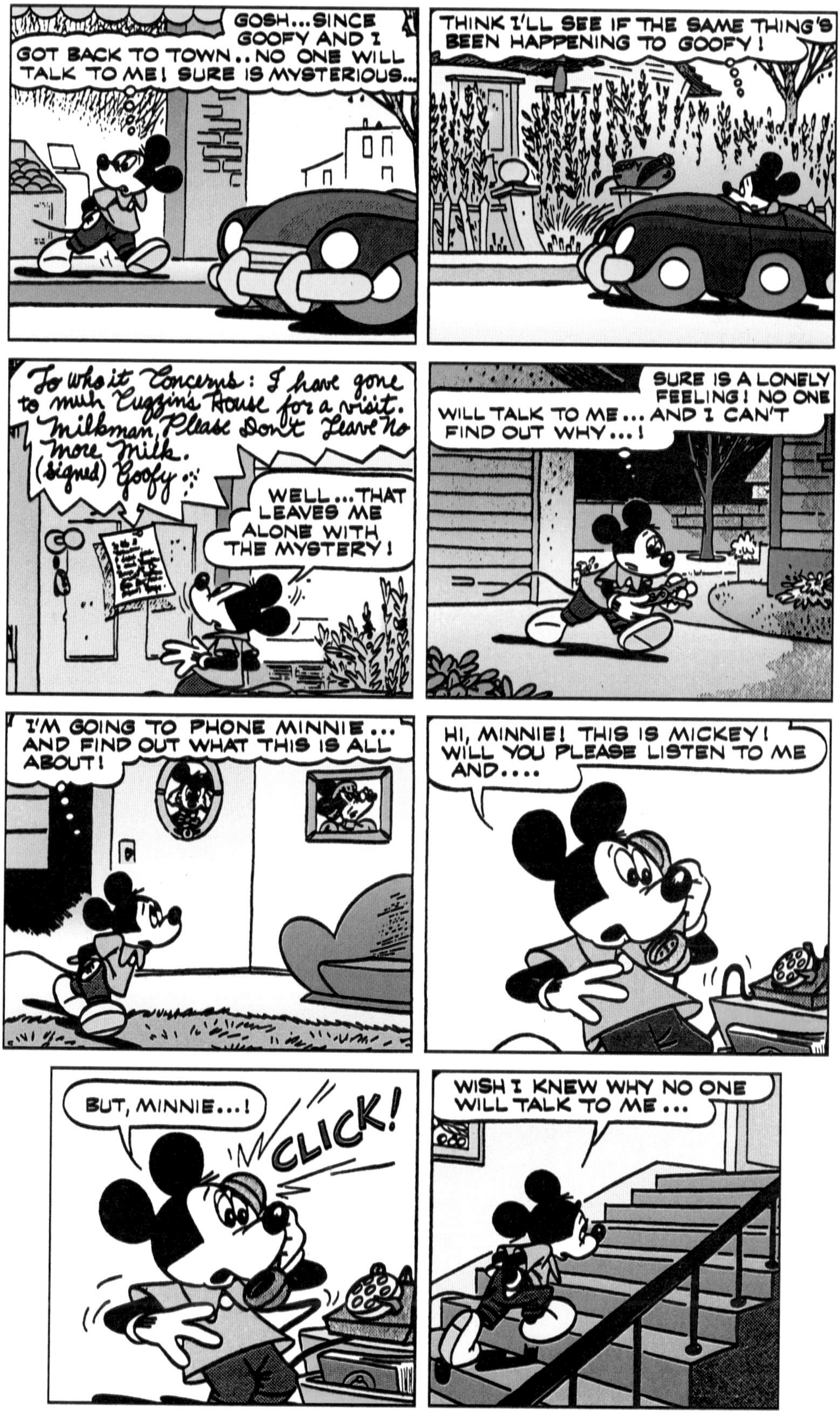
GOSH...SINCE GOOFY AND I GOT BACK TO TOWN..NO ONE WILL TALK TO ME! SURE IS MYSTERIOUS...
THINK I'LL SEE IF THE SAME THING'S BEEN HAPPENING TO GOOFY!
To who it Concerns: I have gone to muh Cuzzin's House for a visit. Milkman, Please Don't Leave No more Milk. (signed) Goofy
WELL...THAT LEAVES ME ALONE WITH THE MYSTERY!
SURE IS A LONELY FEELING! NO ONE WILL TALK TO ME... AND I CAN'T FIND OUT WHY...!
I'M GOING TO PHONE MINNIE... AND FIND OUT WHAT THIS IS ALL ABOUT!
HI, MINNIE! THIS IS MICKEY! WILL YOU PLEASE LISTEN TO ME AND....
BUT, MINNIE...!
CLICK!
WISH I KNEW WHY NO ONE WILL TALK TO ME...

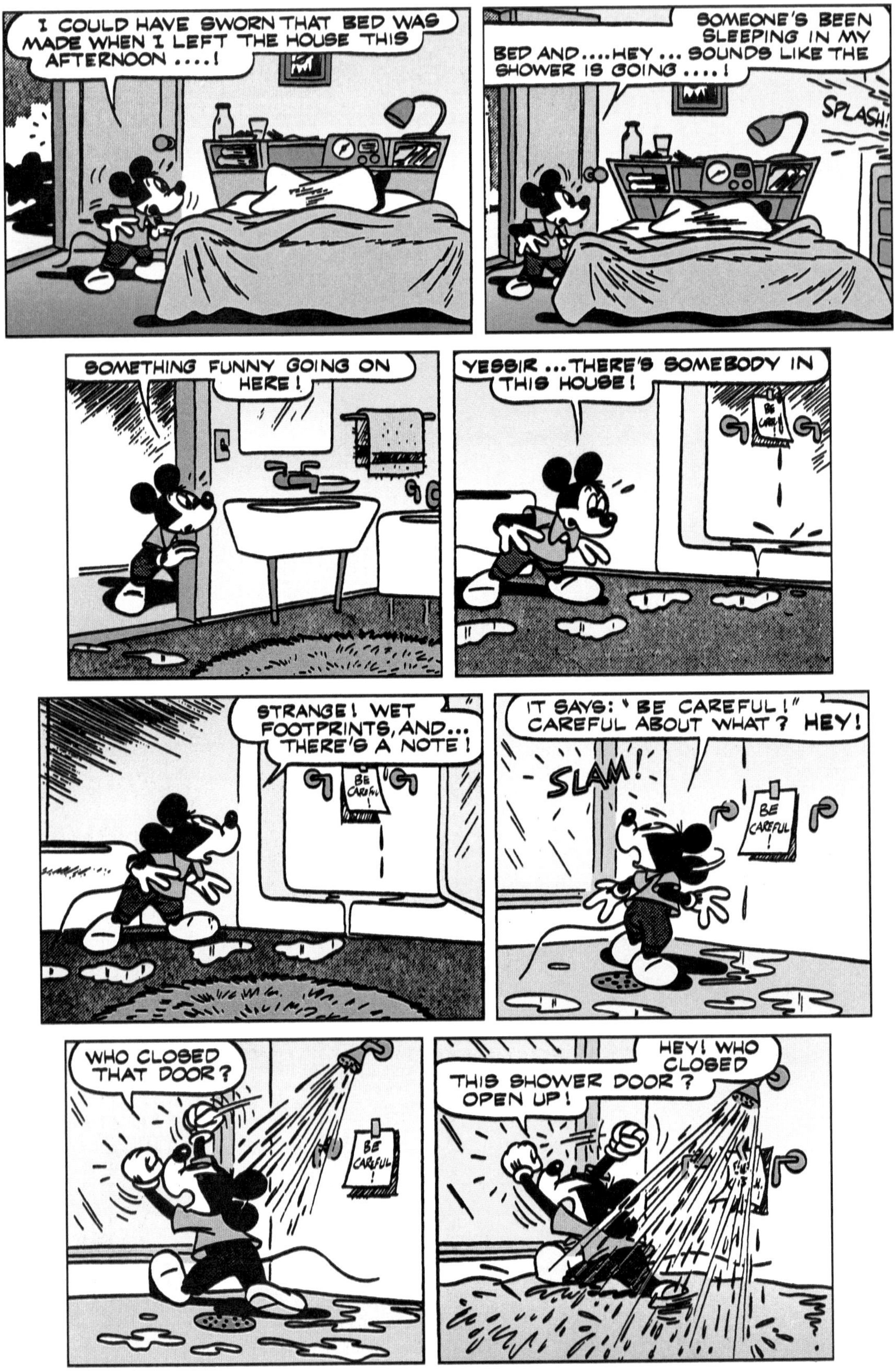
I COULD HAVE SWORN THAT BED WAS MADE WHEN I LEFT THE HOUSE THIS AFTERNOON ....!
SOMEONE'S BEEN SLEEPING IN MY BED AND....HEY ... SOUNDS LIKE THE SHOWER IS GOING ....!
SPLASH!
SOMETHING FUNNY GOING ON HERE!
YESSIR ...THERE'S SOMEBODY IN THIS HOUSE!
BE CAREFUL!
STRANGE! WET FOOTPRINTS, AND... THERE'S A NOTE!
BE CAREFUL !
IT SAYS: "BE CAREFUL!" CAREFUL ABOUT WHAT? HEY!
SLAM!
BE CAREFUL !
WHO CLOSED THAT DOOR?
BE CAREFUL !
HEY! WHO CLOSED THIS SHOWER DOOR? OPEN UP!

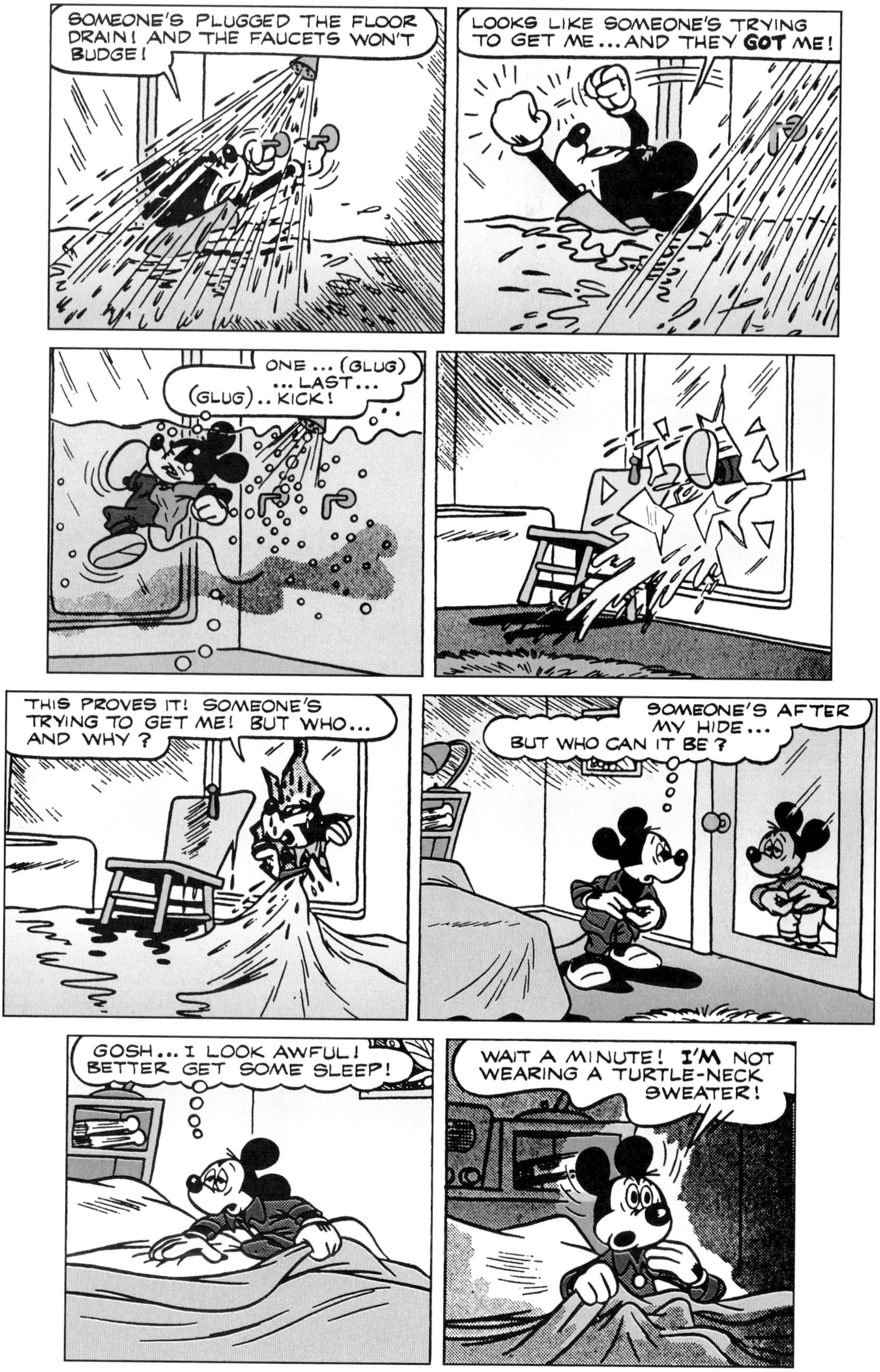
SOMEONE'S PLUGGED THE FLOOR DRAIN! AND THE FAUCETS WON'T BUDGE!
LOOKS LIKE SOMEONE'S TRYING TO GET ME...AND THEY GOT ME!
ONE ... (GLUG) ... LAST... (GLUG).. KICK!
THIS PROVES IT! SOMEONE'S TRYING TO GET ME! BUT WHO... AND WHY?
SOMEONE'S AFTER MY HIDE... BUT WHO CAN IT BE?
GOSH... I LOOK AWFUL! BETTER GET SOME SLEEP!
WAIT A MINUTE! I'M NOT WEARING A TURTLE-NECK SWEATER!

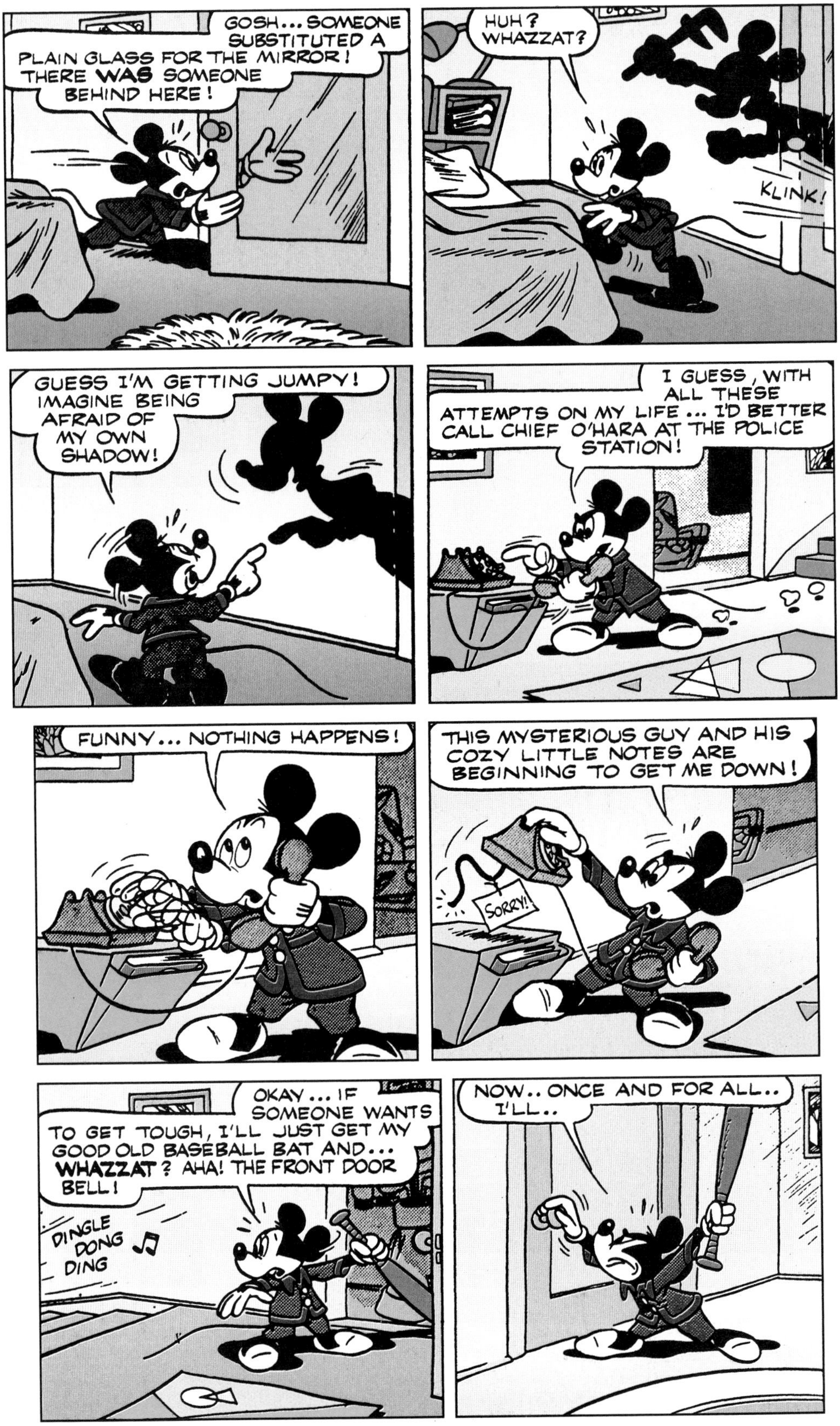
GOSH... SOMEONE SUBSTITUTED A PLAIN GLASS FOR THE MIRROR! THERE WAS SOMEONE BEHIND HERE!
HUH? WHAZZAT?
KLINK!
GUESS I'M GETTING JUMPY! IMAGINE BEING AFRAID OF MY OWN SHADOW!
I GUESS, WITH ALL THESE ATTEMPTS ON MY LIFE... I'D BETTER CALL CHIEF O'HARA AT THE POLICE STATION!
FUNNY... NOTHING HAPPENS!
THIS MYSTERIOUS GUY AND HIS COZY LITTLE NOTES ARE BEGINNING TO GET ME DOWN!
SORRY!
OKAY... IF SOMEONE WANTS TO GET TOUGH, I'LL JUST GET MY GOOD OLD BASEBALL BAT AND... WHAZZAT? AHA! THE FRONT DOOR BELL!
DINGLE DONG DING
NOW.. ONCE AND FOR ALL.. I'LL..

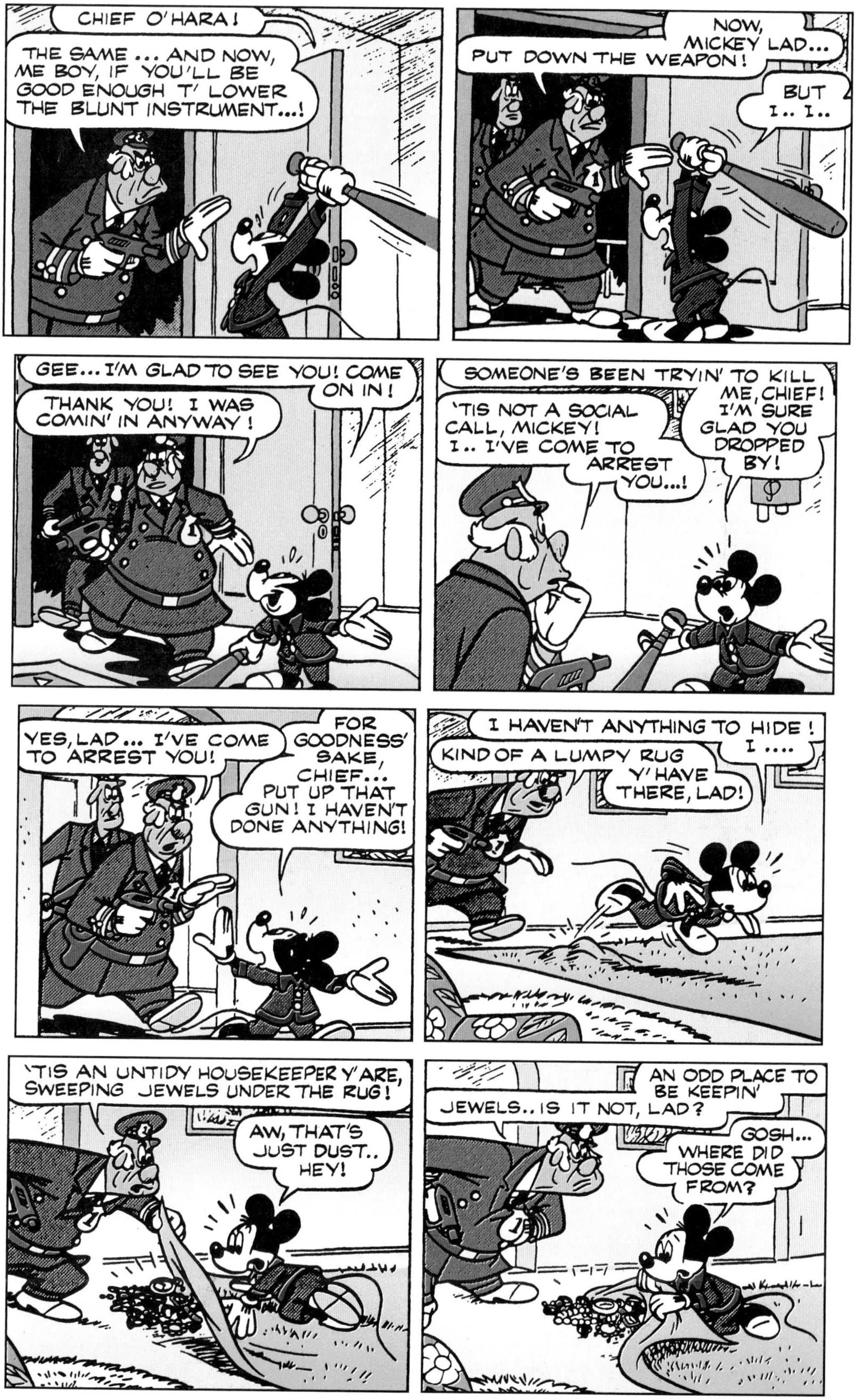

CHIEF O'HARA!
THE SAME ... AND NOW, ME BOY, IF YOU'LL BE GOOD ENOUGH T' LOWER THE BLUNT INSTRUMENT...!
NOW, MICKEY LAD... PUT DOWN THE WEAPON!
BUT I.. I..
GEE... I'M GLAD TO SEE YOU! COME ON IN!
THANK YOU! I WAS COMIN' IN ANYWAY!
SOMEONE'S BEEN TRYIN' TO KILL ME, CHIEF! I'M SURE GLAD YOU DROPPED BY!
'TIS NOT A SOCIAL CALL, MICKEY! I.. I'VE COME TO ARREST YOU...!
YES, LAD... I'VE COME TO ARREST YOU!
FOR GOODNESS' SAKE, CHIEF... PUT UP THAT GUN! I HAVEN'T DONE ANYTHING!
I HAVEN'T ANYTHING TO HIDE! I ....
KIND OF A LUMPY RUG Y' HAVE THERE, LAD!
'TIS AN UNTIDY HOUSEKEEPER Y'ARE, SWEEPING JEWELS UNDER THE RUG!
AW, THAT'S JUST DUST.. HEY!
AN ODD PLACE TO BE KEEPIN' JEWELS.. IS IT NOT, LAD?
GOSH... WHERE DID THOSE COME FROM?

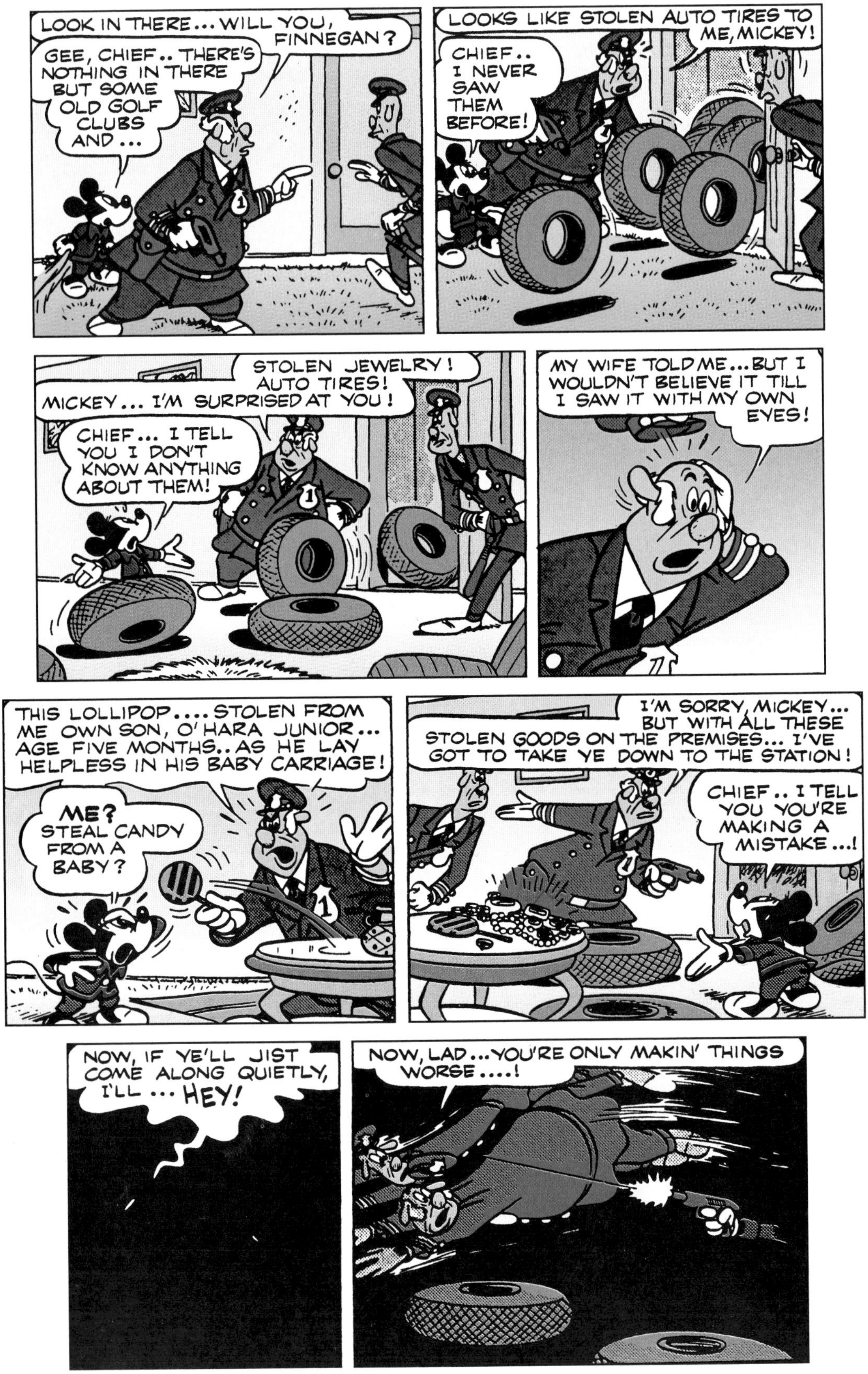
LOOK IN THERE... WILL YOU, FINNEGAN?
GEE, CHIEF.. THERE'S NOTHING IN THERE BUT SOME OLD GOLF CLUBS AND...
LOOKS LIKE STOLEN AUTO TIRES TO ME, MICKEY!
CHIEF.. I NEVER SAW THEM BEFORE!
STOLEN JEWELRY! AUTO TIRES!
MICKEY... I'M SURPRISED AT YOU!
CHIEF... I TELL YOU I DON'T KNOW ANYTHING ABOUT THEM!
MY WIFE TOLD ME... BUT I WOULDN'T BELIEVE IT TILL I SAW IT WITH MY OWN EYES!
THIS LOLLIPOP.... STOLEN FROM ME OWN SON, O'HARA JUNIOR... AGE FIVE MONTHS.. AS HE LAY HELPLESS IN HIS BABY CARRIAGE!
ME? STEAL CANDY FROM A BABY?
I'M SORRY, MICKEY... BUT WITH ALL THESE STOLEN GOODS ON THE PREMISES... I'VE GOT TO TAKE YE DOWN TO THE STATION!
CHIEF.. I TELL YOU YOU'RE MAKING A MISTAKE...!
NOW, IF YE'LL JIST COME ALONG QUIETLY, I'LL... HEY!
NOW, LAD... YOU'RE ONLY MAKIN' THINGS WORSE....!

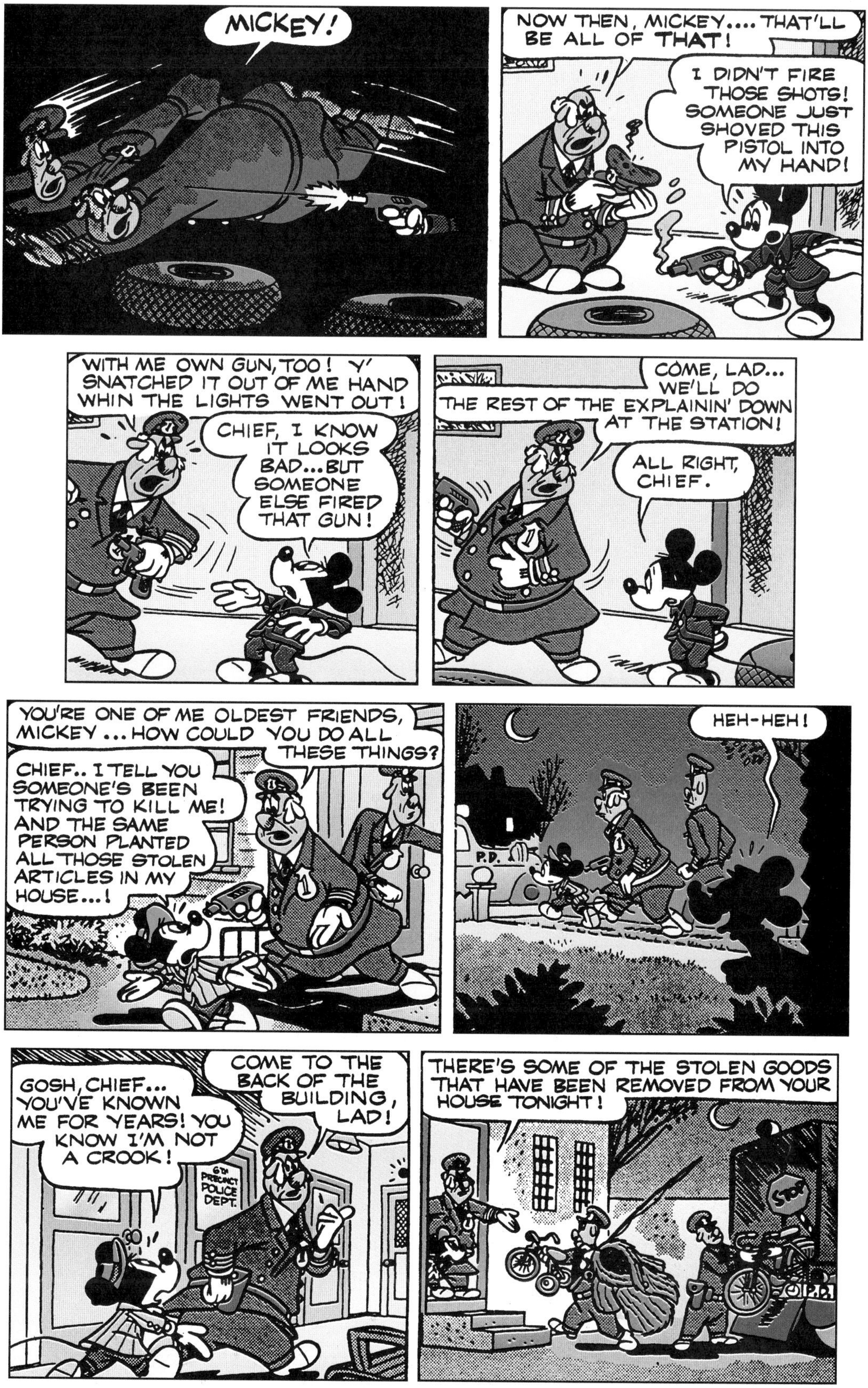
MICKEY!
NOW THEN, MICKEY.... THAT'LL BE ALL OF THAT!
I DIDN'T FIRE THOSE SHOTS! SOMEONE JUST SHOVED THIS PISTOL INTO MY HAND!
WITH ME OWN GUN, TOO! Y' SNATCHED IT OUT OF ME HAND WHIN THE LIGHTS WENT OUT!
CHIEF, I KNOW IT LOOKS BAD...BUT SOMEONE ELSE FIRED THAT GUN!
COME, LAD... WE'LL DO THE REST OF THE EXPLAININ' DOWN AT THE STATION!
ALL RIGHT, CHIEF.
YOU'RE ONE OF ME OLDEST FRIENDS, MICKEY ... HOW COULD YOU DO ALL THESE THINGS?
CHIEF.. I TELL YOU SOMEONE'S BEEN TRYING TO KILL ME! AND THE SAME PERSON PLANTED ALL THOSE STOLEN ARTICLES IN MY HOUSE...!
P.D.
HEH-HEH!
GOSH, CHIEF... YOU'VE KNOWN ME FOR YEARS! YOU KNOW I'M NOT A CROOK!
COME TO THE BACK OF THE BUILDING, LAD!
6TH PRECINCT POLICE DEPT.
THERE'S SOME OF THE STOLEN GOODS THAT HAVE BEEN REMOVED FROM YOUR HOUSE TONIGHT!
STOP
P.D.

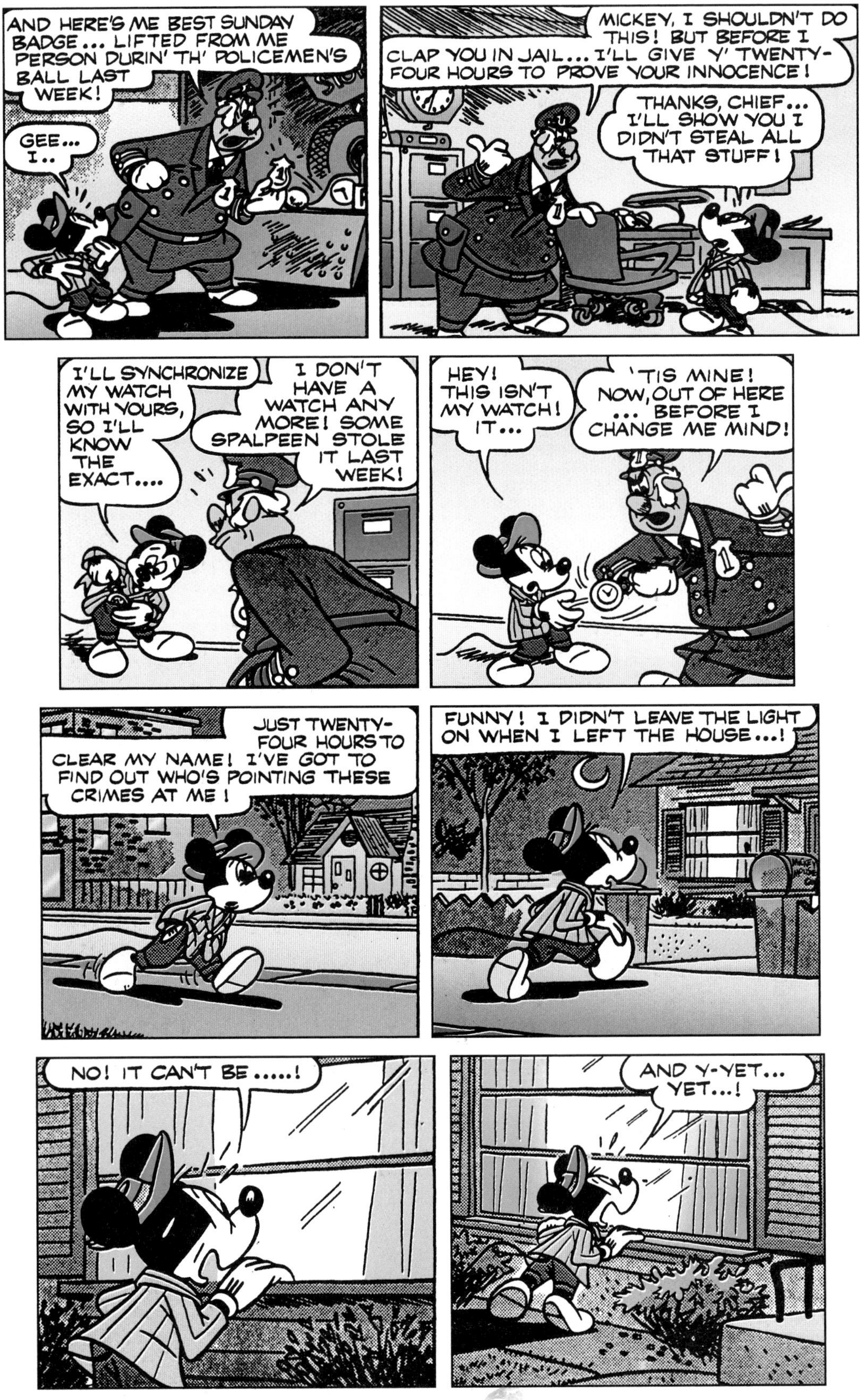
AND HERE'S ME BEST SUNDAY BADGE... LIFTED FROM ME PERSON DURIN' TH' POLICEMEN'S BALL LAST WEEK!
GEE... I..
MICKEY, I SHOULDN'T DO THIS! BUT BEFORE I CLAP YOU IN JAIL... I'LL GIVE Y' TWENTY-FOUR HOURS TO PROVE YOUR INNOCENCE!
THANKS, CHIEF... I'LL SHOW YOU I DIDN'T STEAL ALL THAT STUFF!
I'LL SYNCHRONIZE MY WATCH WITH YOURS, SO I'LL KNOW THE EXACT....
I DON'T HAVE A WATCH ANY MORE! SOME SPALPEEN STOLE IT LAST WEEK!
HEY! THIS ISN'T MY WATCH! IT...
'TIS MINE! NOW, OUT OF HERE ... BEFORE I CHANGE ME MIND!
JUST TWENTY-FOUR HOURS TO CLEAR MY NAME! I'VE GOT TO FIND OUT WHO'S POINTING THESE CRIMES AT ME!
FUNNY! I DIDN'T LEAVE THE LIGHT ON WHEN I LEFT THE HOUSE...!
NO! IT CAN'T BE .....!
AND Y-YET... YET...!

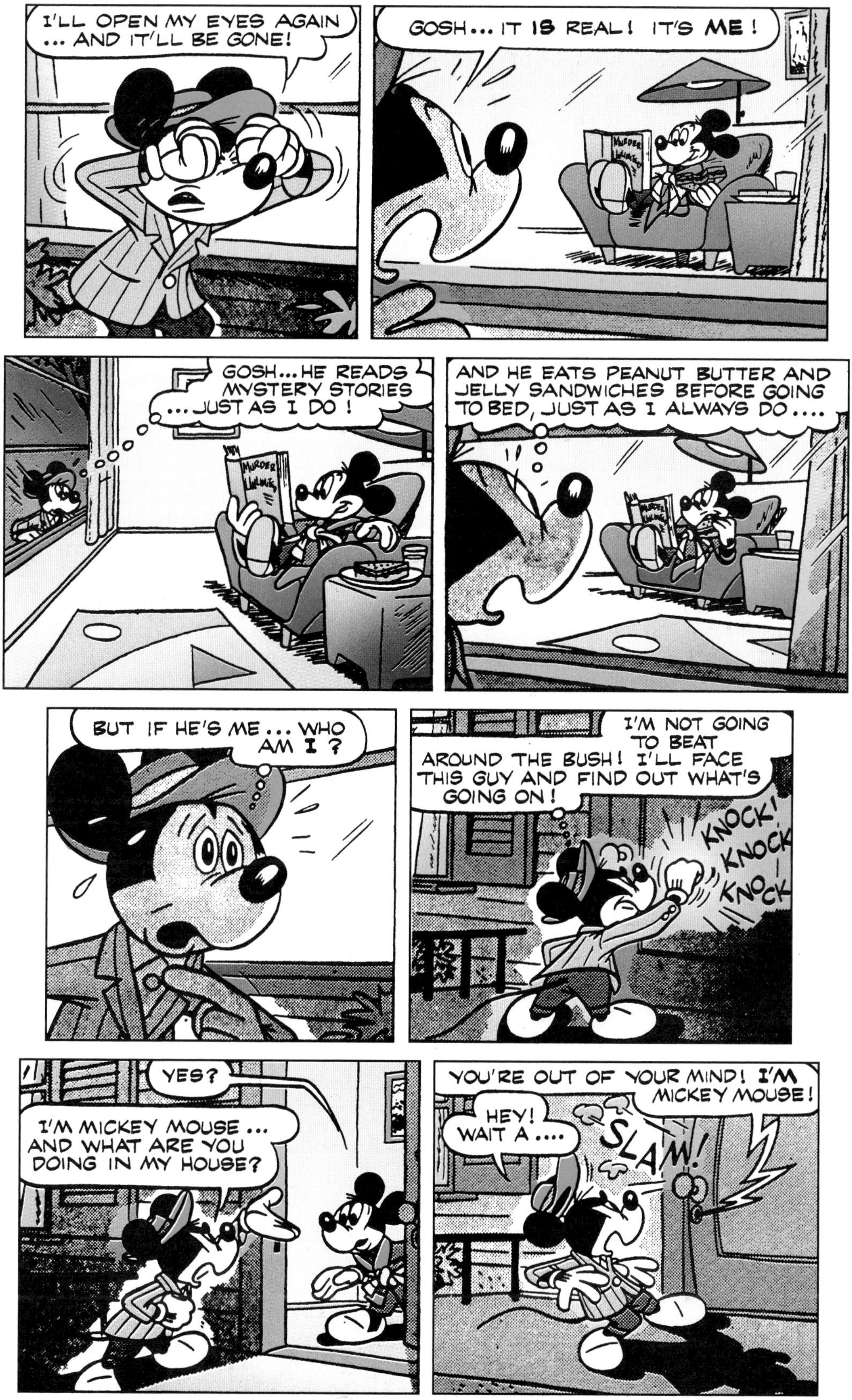
I'LL OPEN MY EYES AGAIN ... AND IT'LL BE GONE!
GOSH... IT IS REAL! IT'S ME!
MURDER UNLIMITED
GOSH... HE READS MYSTERY STORIES ... JUST AS I DO!
AND HE EATS PEANUT BUTTER AND JELLY SANDWICHES BEFORE GOING TO BED, JUST AS I ALWAYS DO....
BUT IF HE'S ME... WHO AM I?
I'M NOT GOING TO BEAT AROUND THE BUSH! I'LL FACE THIS GUY AND FIND OUT WHAT'S GOING ON!
KNOCK! KNOCK! KNOCK
YES?
I'M MICKEY MOUSE... AND WHAT ARE YOU DOING IN MY HOUSE?
YOU'RE OUT OF YOUR MIND! I'M MICKEY MOUSE!
HEY! WAIT A....
SLAM!

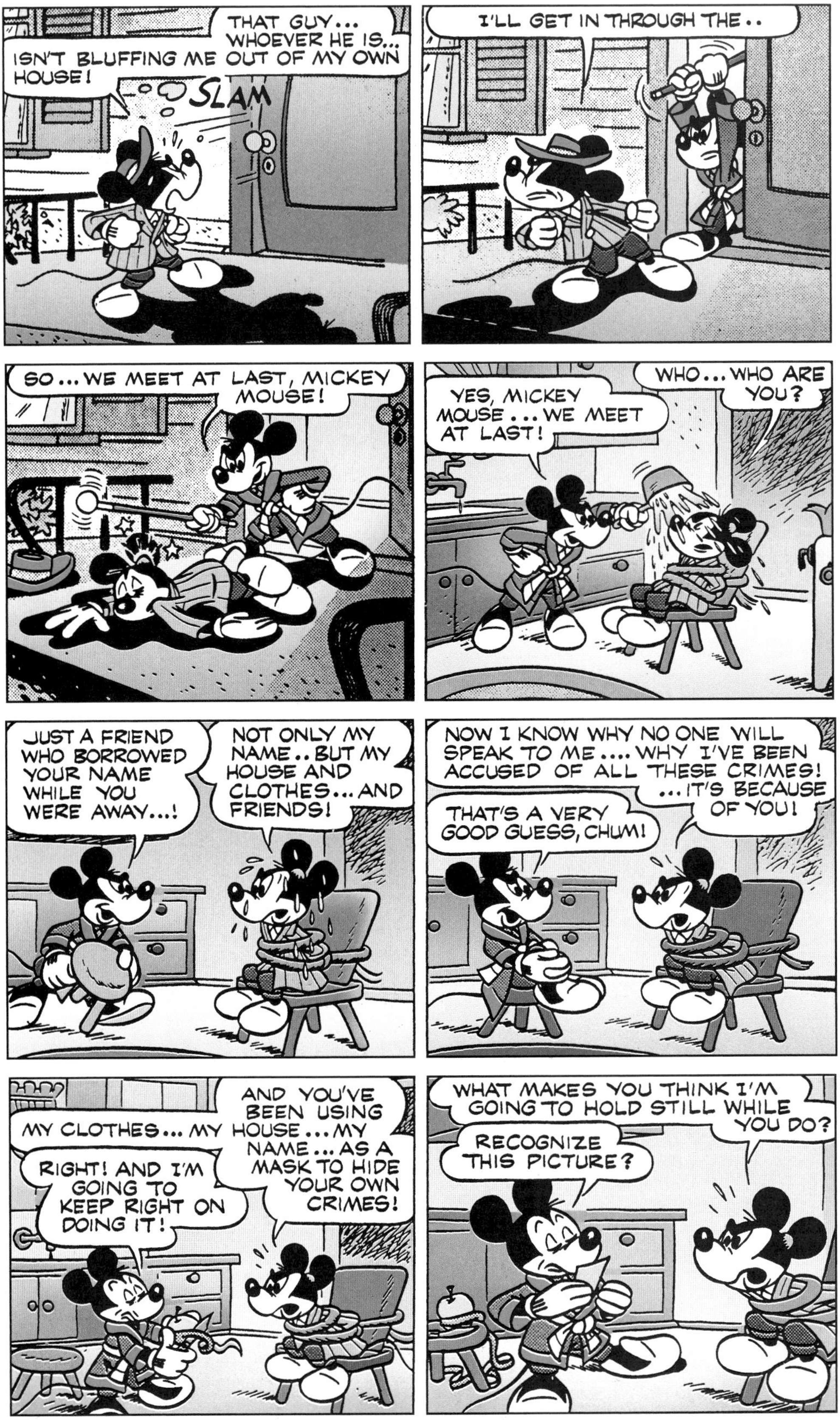
THAT GUY... WHOEVER HE IS... ISN'T BLUFFING ME OUT OF MY OWN HOUSE!
SLAM
I'LL GET IN THROUGH THE..
SO... WE MEET AT LAST, MICKEY MOUSE!
WHO... WHO ARE YOU?
YES, MICKEY MOUSE... WE MEET AT LAST!
JUST A FRIEND WHO BORROWED YOUR NAME WHILE YOU WERE AWAY...!
NOT ONLY MY NAME.. BUT MY HOUSE AND CLOTHES... AND FRIENDS!
NOW I KNOW WHY NO ONE WILL SPEAK TO ME.... WHY I'VE BEEN ACCUSED OF ALL THESE CRIMES! ...IT'S BECAUSE OF YOU!
THAT'S A VERY GOOD GUESS, CHUM!
MY CLOTHES... MY HOUSE... MY NAME... AS A MASK TO HIDE YOUR OWN CRIMES!
AND YOU'VE BEEN USING
RIGHT! AND I'M GOING TO KEEP RIGHT ON DOING IT!
WHAT MAKES YOU THINK I'M GOING TO HOLD STILL WHILE YOU DO?
RECOGNIZE THIS PICTURE?

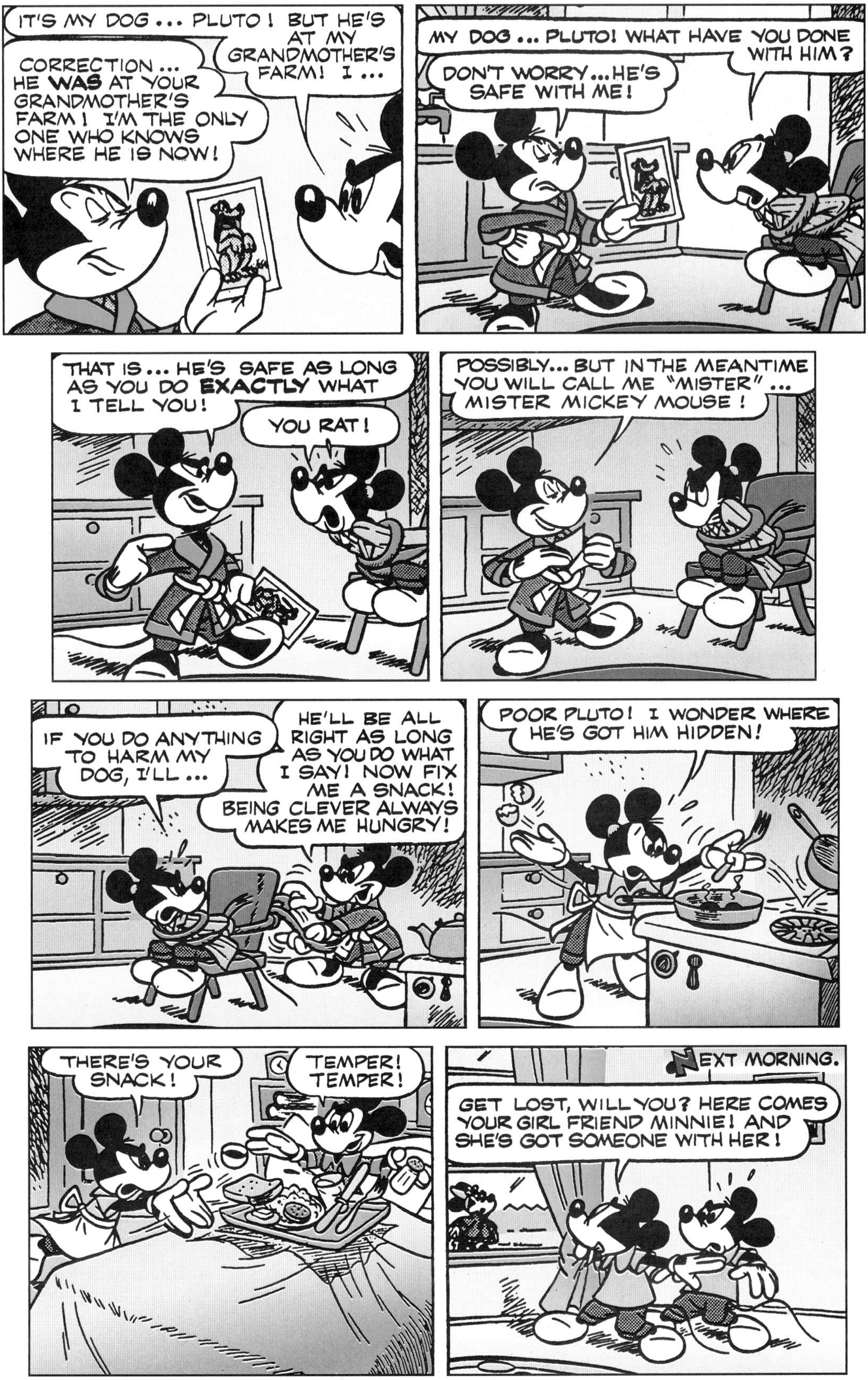
IT'S MY DOG ... PLUTO! BUT HE'S AT MY GRANDMOTHER'S FARM! I ...
CORRECTION ... HE WAS AT YOUR GRANDMOTHER'S FARM! I'M THE ONLY ONE WHO KNOWS WHERE HE IS NOW!
MY DOG ... PLUTO! WHAT HAVE YOU DONE WITH HIM?
DON'T WORRY ... HE'S SAFE WITH ME!
THAT IS ... HE'S SAFE AS LONG AS YOU DO EXACTLY WHAT I TELL YOU!
YOU RAT!
POSSIBLY ... BUT IN THE MEANTIME YOU WILL CALL ME "MISTER" ... MISTER MICKEY MOUSE!
IF YOU DO ANYTHING TO HARM MY DOG, I'LL ...
HE'LL BE ALL RIGHT AS LONG AS YOU DO WHAT I SAY! NOW FIX ME A SNACK! BEING CLEVER ALWAYS MAKES ME HUNGRY!
POOR PLUTO! I WONDER WHERE HE'S GOT HIM HIDDEN!
THERE'S YOUR SNACK!
TEMPER! TEMPER!
NEXT MORNING.
GET LOST, WILL YOU? HERE COMES YOUR GIRL FRIEND MINNIE! AND SHE'S GOT SOMEONE WITH HER!

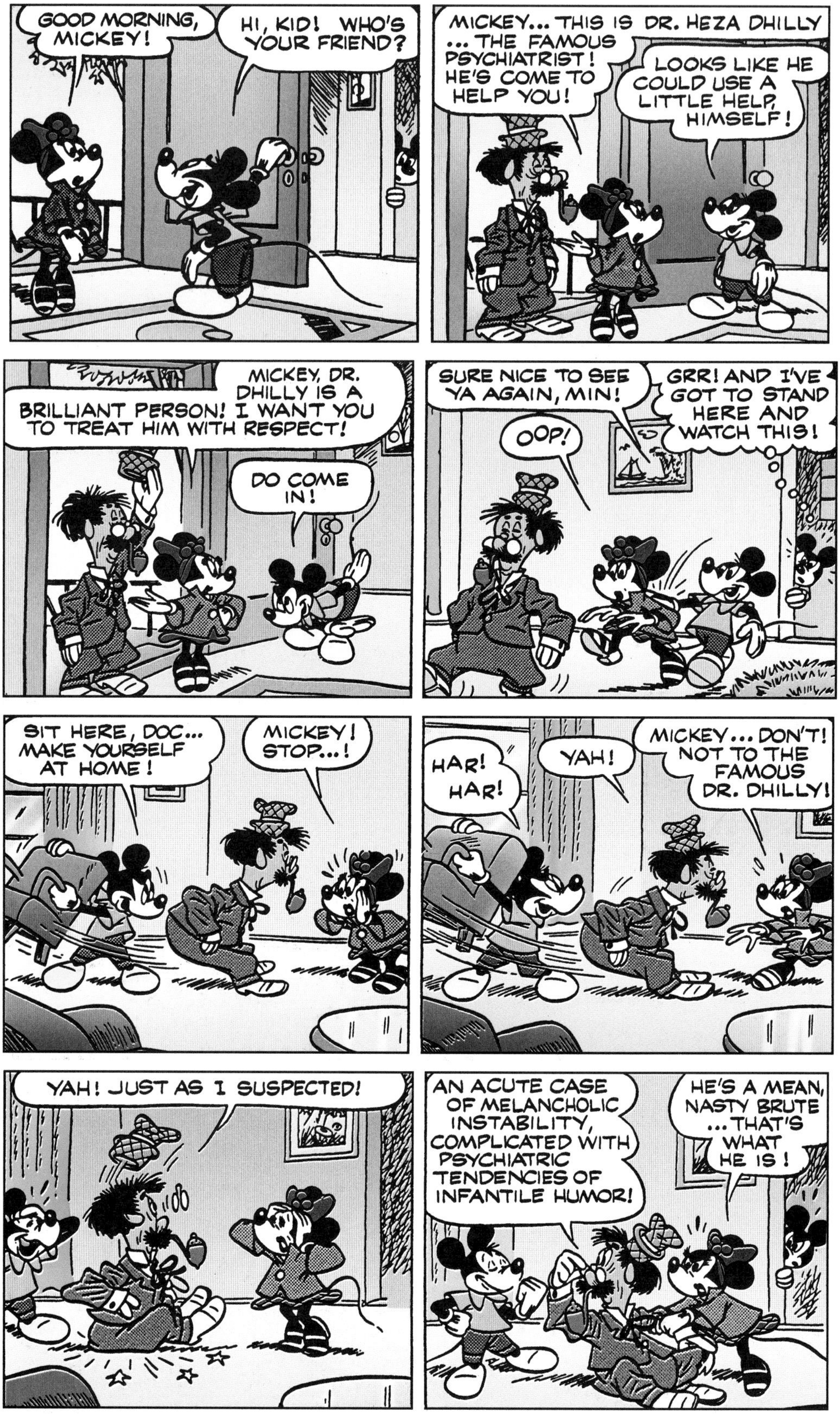
GOOD MORNING, MICKEY!
HI, KID! WHO'S YOUR FRIEND?
MICKEY... THIS IS DR. HEZA DHILLY ... THE FAMOUS PSYCHIATRIST! HE'S COME TO HELP YOU!
LOOKS LIKE HE COULD USE A LITTLE HELP, HIMSELF!
MICKEY, DR. DHILLY IS A BRILLIANT PERSON! I WANT YOU TO TREAT HIM WITH RESPECT!
DO COME IN!
SURE NICE TO SEE YA AGAIN, MIN!
OOP!
GRR! AND I'VE GOT TO STAND HERE AND WATCH THIS!
SIT HERE, DOC... MAKE YOURSELF AT HOME!
MICKEY! STOP...!
HAR! HAR!
YAH!
MICKEY... DON'T! NOT TO THE FAMOUS DR. DHILLY!
YAH! JUST AS I SUSPECTED!
AN ACUTE CASE OF MELANCHOLIC INSTABILITY, COMPLICATED WITH PSYCHIATRIC TENDENCIES OF INFANTILE HUMOR!
HE'S A MEAN, NASTY BRUTE ...THAT'S WHAT HE IS!

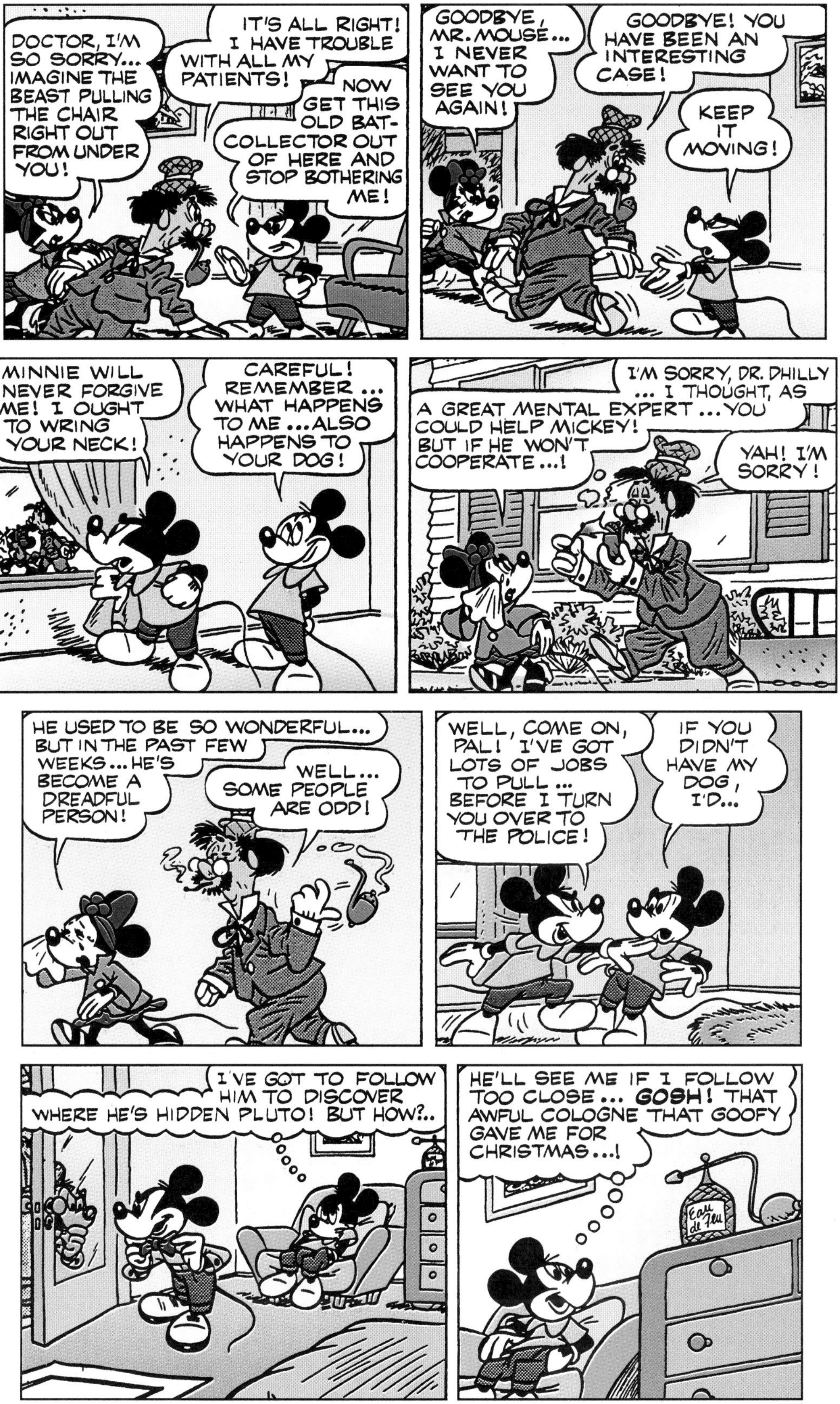
DOCTOR, I'M SO SORRY... IMAGINE THE BEAST PULLING THE CHAIR RIGHT OUT FROM UNDER YOU!
IT'S ALL RIGHT! I HAVE TROUBLE WITH ALL MY PATIENTS!
NOW GET THIS OLD BAT-COLLECTOR OUT OF HERE AND STOP BOTHERING ME!
GOODBYE, MR. MOUSE... I NEVER WANT TO SEE YOU AGAIN!
GOODBYE! YOU HAVE BEEN AN INTERESTING CASE!
KEEP IT MOVING!
MINNIE WILL NEVER FORGIVE ME! I OUGHT TO WRING YOUR NECK!
CAREFUL! REMEMBER... WHAT HAPPENS TO ME... ALSO HAPPENS TO YOUR DOG!
I'M SORRY, DR. DHILLY ... I THOUGHT, AS A GREAT MENTAL EXPERT ... YOU COULD HELP MICKEY! BUT IF HE WON'T COOPERATE...!
YAH! I'M SORRY!
HE USED TO BE SO WONDERFUL... BUT IN THE PAST FEW WEEKS... HE'S BECOME A DREADFUL PERSON!
WELL... SOME PEOPLE ARE ODD!
WELL, COME ON, PAL! I'VE GOT LOTS OF JOBS TO PULL... BEFORE I TURN YOU OVER TO THE POLICE!
IF YOU DIDN'T HAVE MY DOG, I'D...!
I'VE GOT TO FOLLOW HIM TO DISCOVER WHERE HE'S HIDDEN PLUTO! BUT HOW?..
HE'LL SEE ME IF I FOLLOW TOO CLOSE... GOSH! THAT AWFUL COLOGNE THAT GOOFY GAVE ME FOR CHRISTMAS...!
Eau de Feu

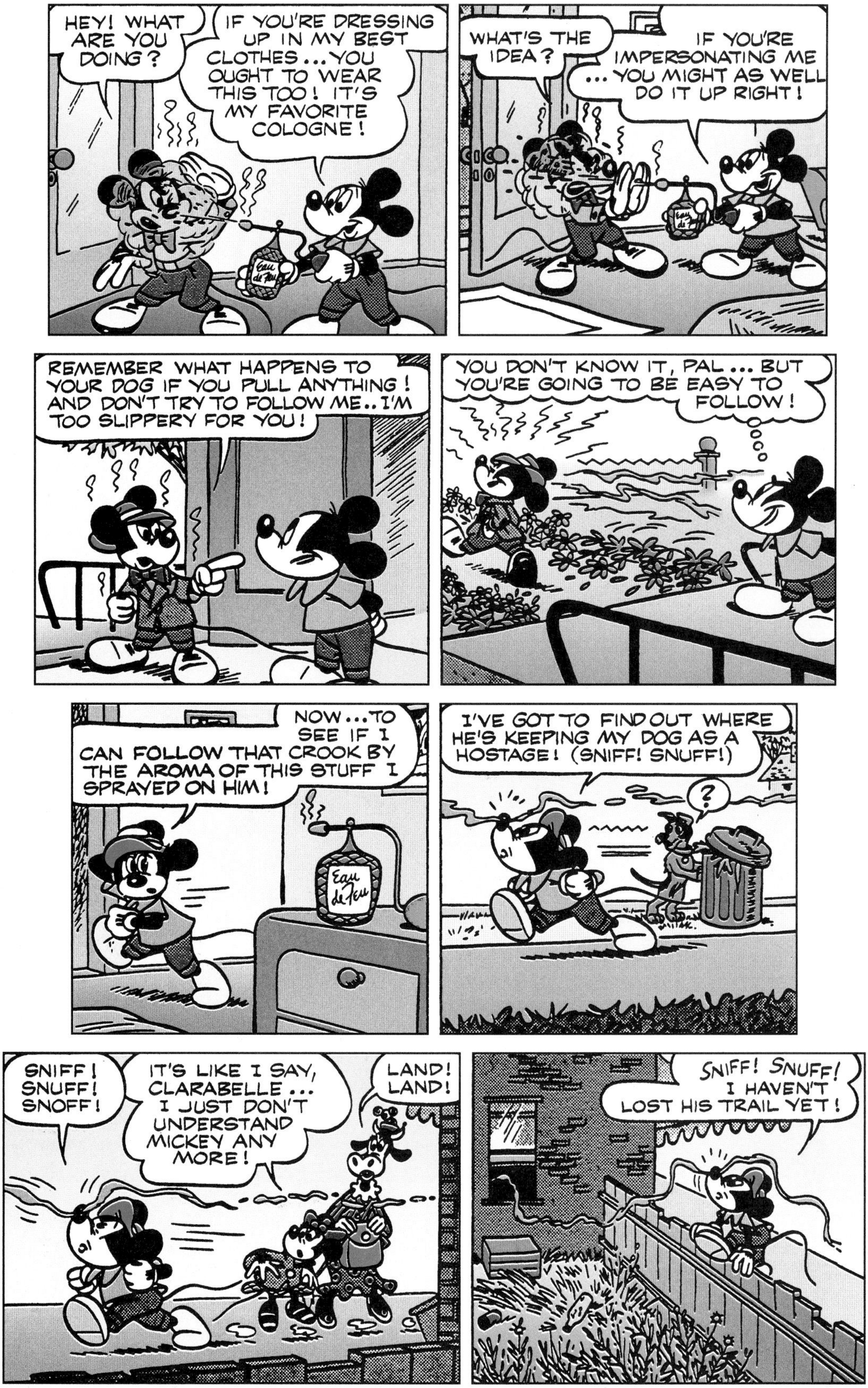
HEY! WHAT ARE YOU DOING?
IF YOU'RE DRESSING UP IN MY BEST CLOTHES... YOU OUGHT TO WEAR THIS TOO! IT'S MY FAVORITE COLOGNE!
Eau de Feu
WHAT'S THE IDEA?
IF YOU'RE IMPERSONATING ME ... YOU MIGHT AS WELL DO IT UP RIGHT!
REMEMBER WHAT HAPPENS TO YOUR DOG IF YOU PULL ANYTHING! AND DON'T TRY TO FOLLOW ME.. I'M TOO SLIPPERY FOR YOU!
YOU DON'T KNOW IT, PAL... BUT YOU'RE GOING TO BE EASY TO FOLLOW!
NOW...TO SEE IF I CAN FOLLOW THAT CROOK BY THE AROMA OF THIS STUFF I SPRAYED ON HIM!
Eau de Feu
I'VE GOT TO FIND OUT WHERE HE'S KEEPING MY DOG AS A HOSTAGE! (SNIFF! SNUFF!)
?
SNIFF! SNUFF! SNOFF!
IT'S LIKE I SAY, CLARABELLE... I JUST DON'T UNDERSTAND MICKEY ANY MORE!
LAND! LAND!
SNIFF! SNUFF! I HAVEN'T LOST HIS TRAIL YET!

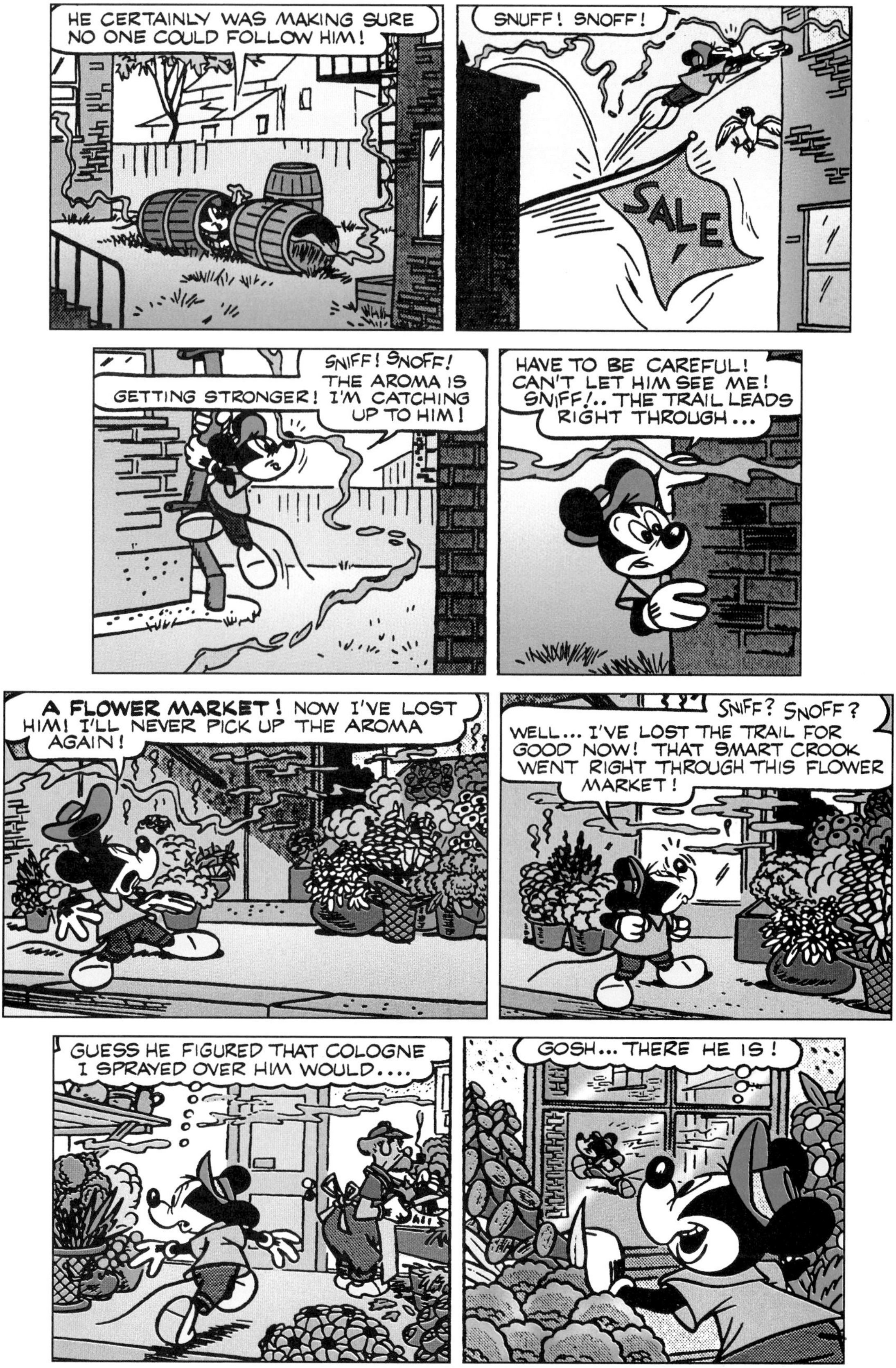
HE CERTAINLY WAS MAKING SURE NO ONE COULD FOLLOW HIM!
SNUFF! SNOFF!
SALE
SNIFF! SNOFF! THE AROMA IS GETTING STRONGER! I'M CATCHING UP TO HIM!
HAVE TO BE CAREFUL! CAN'T LET HIM SEE ME! SNIFF!.. THE TRAIL LEADS RIGHT THROUGH...
A FLOWER MARKET! NOW I'VE LOST HIM! I'LL NEVER PICK UP THE AROMA AGAIN!
SNIFF? SNOFF? WELL... I'VE LOST THE TRAIL FOR GOOD NOW! THAT SMART CROOK WENT RIGHT THROUGH THIS FLOWER MARKET!
GUESS HE FIGURED THAT COLOGNE I SPRAYED OVER HIM WOULD....
GOSH... THERE HE IS!

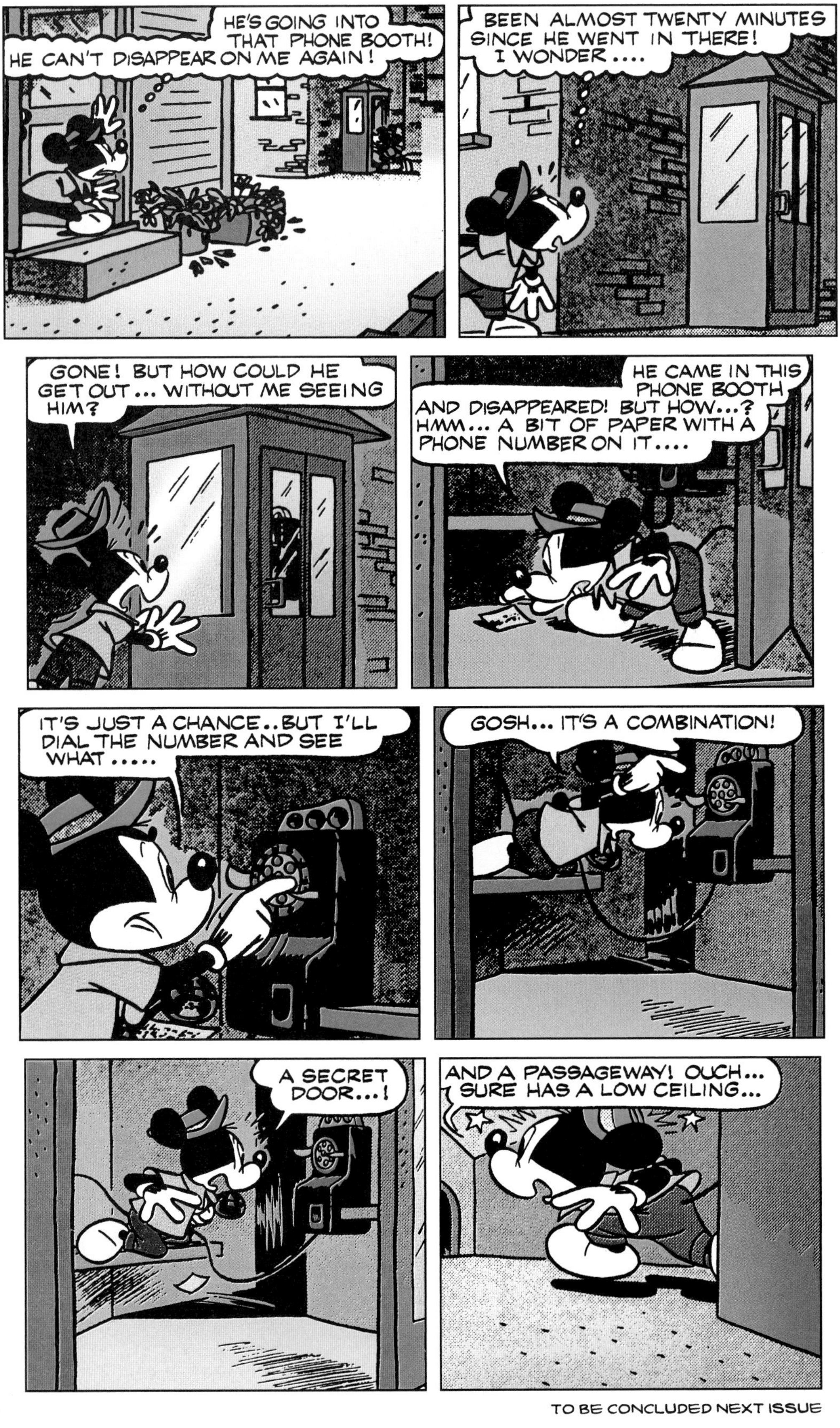
HE'S GOING INTO THAT PHONE BOOTH!
HE CAN'T DISAPPEAR ON ME AGAIN!
BEEN ALMOST TWENTY MINUTES SINCE HE WENT IN THERE! I WONDER....
GONE! BUT HOW COULD HE GET OUT... WITHOUT ME SEEING HIM?
HE CAME IN THIS PHONE BOOTH AND DISAPPEARED! BUT HOW...? HMM... A BIT OF PAPER WITH A PHONE NUMBER ON IT....
IT'S JUST A CHANCE..BUT I'LL DIAL THE NUMBER AND SEE WHAT.....
GOSH... IT'S A COMBINATION!
A SECRET DOOR...!
AND A PASSAGEWAY! OUCH... SURE HAS A LOW CEILING...

TO BE CONCLUDED NEXT ISSUE

Uncle Scrooge is in another bind. Can Donald and the boys save him from the Peeweegahs? ("What's a Peeweegah," you ask?)

UH OH!

©2007 Disney Enterprises, Inc.

Learn all about Peeweegahs and Wendigos in *Walt Disney's Uncle Scrooge Adventures—The Barks/Rosa Collection*. This new series features stories by famed writers/illustrators Carl Barks and Don Rosa. Each volume contains an original Carl Barks classic followed by a Don Rosa sequel. Volume One kicks things off with "Land of the Pygmy Indians" and "War of the Wendigo."

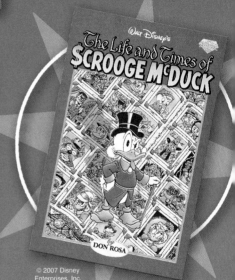

Walt Disney's Grandma Duck in Cock-a-Doodle Don't

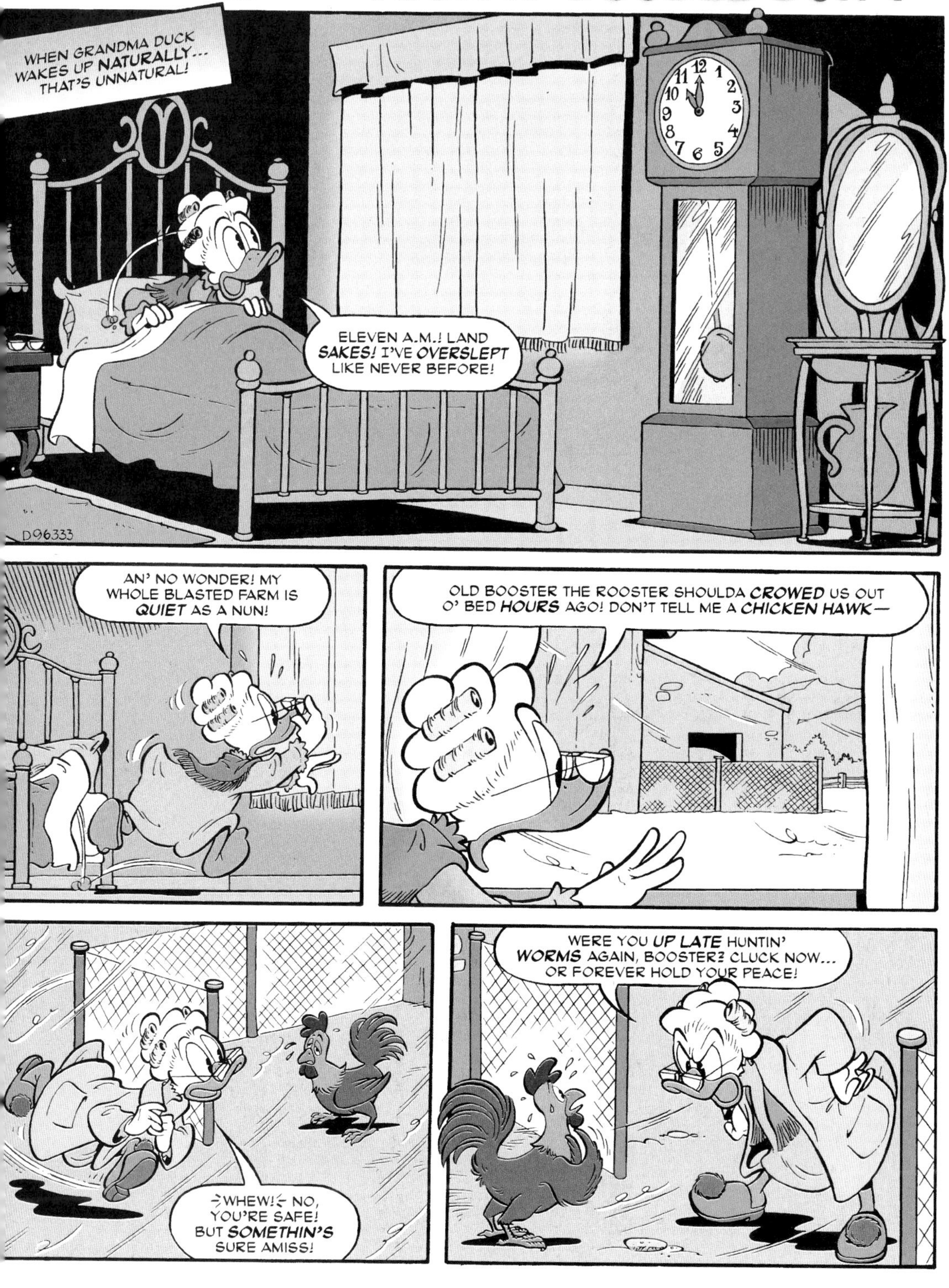
WHEN GRANDMA DUCK WAKES UP NATURALLY... THAT'S UNNATURAL!
ELEVEN A.M.! LAND SAKES! I'VE OVERSLEPT LIKE NEVER BEFORE!
D96333
AN' NO WONDER! MY WHOLE BLASTED FARM IS QUIET AS A NUN!
OLD BOOSTER THE ROOSTER SHOULDA CROWED US OUT O' BED HOURS AGO! DON'T TELL ME A CHICKEN HAWK—
WHEW! NO, YOU'RE SAFE! BUT SOMETHIN'S SURE AMISS!
WERE YOU UP LATE HUNTIN' WORMS AGAIN, BOOSTER? CLUCK NOW... OR FOREVER HOLD YOUR PEACE!

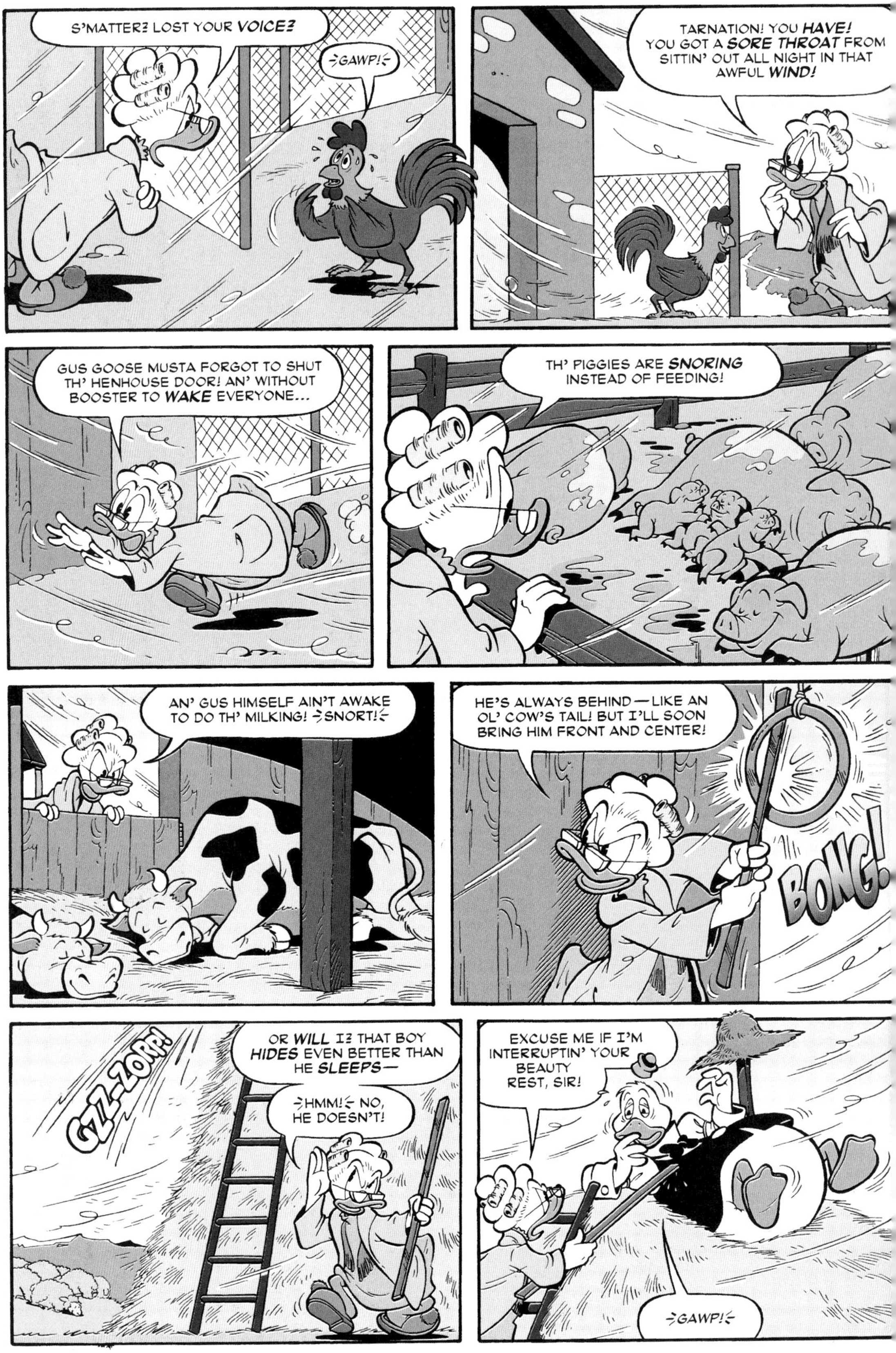
S'MATTER? LOST YOUR VOICE?
GAWP!
TARNATION! YOU HAVE! YOU GOT A SORE THROAT FROM SITTIN' OUT ALL NIGHT IN THAT AWFUL WIND!
GUS GOOSE MUSTA FORGOT TO SHUT TH' HENHOUSE DOOR! AN' WITHOUT BOOSTER TO WAKE EVERYONE...
TH' PIGGIES ARE SNORING INSTEAD OF FEEDING!
AN' GUS HIMSELF AIN'T AWAKE TO DO TH' MILKING! SNORT!
HE'S ALWAYS BEHIND — LIKE AN OL' COW'S TAIL! BUT I'LL SOON BRING HIM FRONT AND CENTER!
BONG!
GZZ-ZORP!
OR WILL I? THAT BOY HIDES EVEN BETTER THAN HE SLEEPS—
HMM! NO, HE DOESN'T!
EXCUSE ME IF I'M INTERRUPTIN' YOUR BEAUTY REST, SIR!
GAWP!

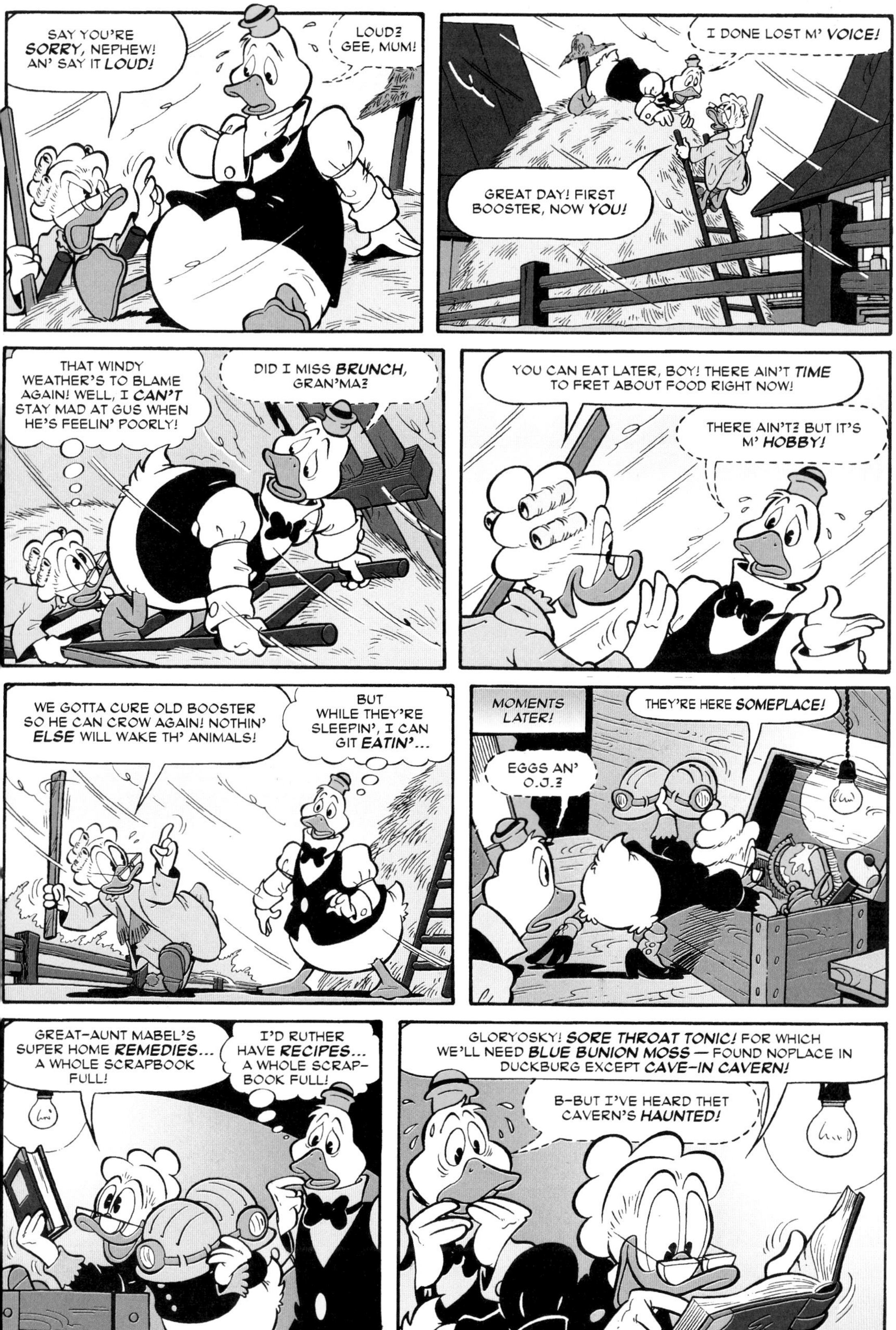
SAY YOU'RE SORRY, NEPHEW! AN' SAY IT LOUD!
LOUD? GEE, MUM!
I DONE LOST M' VOICE!
GREAT DAY! FIRST BOOSTER, NOW YOU!
THAT WINDY WEATHER'S TO BLAME AGAIN! WELL, I CAN'T STAY MAD AT GUS WHEN HE'S FEELIN' POORLY!
DID I MISS BRUNCH, GRAN'MA?
YOU CAN EAT LATER, BOY! THERE AIN'T TIME TO FRET ABOUT FOOD RIGHT NOW!
THERE AIN'T? BUT IT'S M' HOBBY!
WE GOTTA CURE OLD BOOSTER SO HE CAN CROW AGAIN! NOTHIN' ELSE WILL WAKE TH' ANIMALS!
BUT WHILE THEY'RE SLEEPIN', I CAN GIT EATIN'...
MOMENTS LATER!
THEY'RE HERE SOMEPLACE!
EGGS AN' O.J.?
GREAT-AUNT MABEL'S SUPER HOME REMEDIES... A WHOLE SCRAPBOOK FULL!
I'D RUTHER HAVE RECIPES... A WHOLE SCRAP-BOOK FULL!
GLORYOSKY! SORE THROAT TONIC! FOR WHICH WE'LL NEED BLUE BUNION MOSS — FOUND NOPLACE IN DUCKBURG EXCEPT CAVE-IN CAVERN!
B-BUT I'VE HEARD THET CAVERN'S HAUNTED!

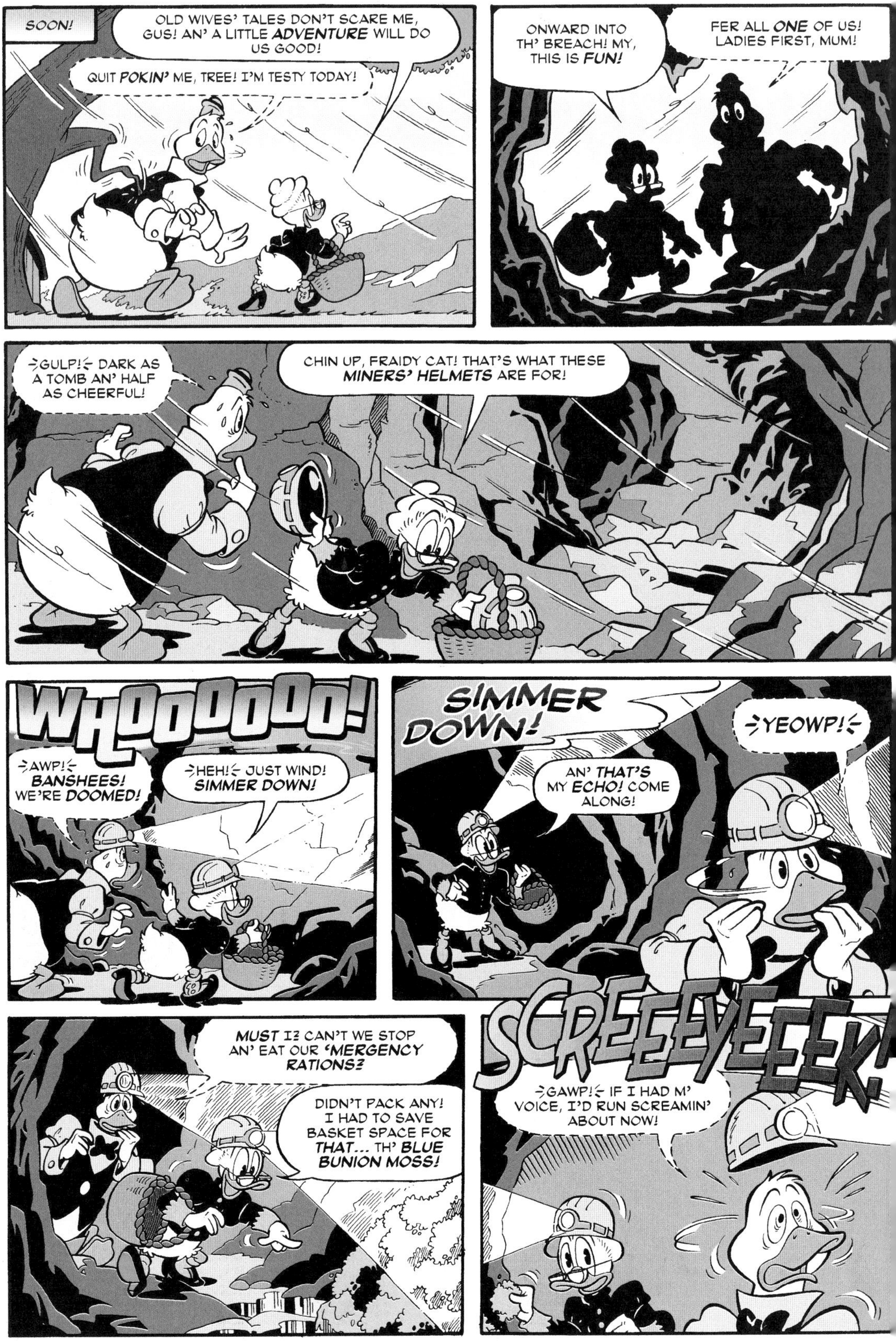
SOON!
OLD WIVES' TALES DON'T SCARE ME, GUS! AN' A LITTLE ADVENTURE WILL DO US GOOD!
QUIT POKIN' ME, TREE! I'M TESTY TODAY!
ONWARD INTO TH' BREACH! MY, THIS IS FUN!
FER ALL ONE OF US! LADIES FIRST, MUM!
GULP! DARK AS A TOMB AN' HALF AS CHEERFUL!
CHIN UP, FRAIDY CAT! THAT'S WHAT THESE MINERS' HELMETS ARE FOR!
WHOOOOOOO!
AWP! BANSHEES! WE'RE DOOMED!
HEH! JUST WIND! SIMMER DOWN!
SIMMER DOWN!
AN' THAT'S MY ECHO! COME ALONG!
YEOWP!
MUST I? CAN'T WE STOP AN' EAT OUR 'MERGENCY RATIONS?
DIDN'T PACK ANY! I HAD TO SAVE BASKET SPACE FOR THAT... TH' BLUE BUNION MOSS!
SCREEEYEEEK!
GAWP! IF I HAD M' VOICE, I'D RUN SCREAMIN' ABOUT NOW!

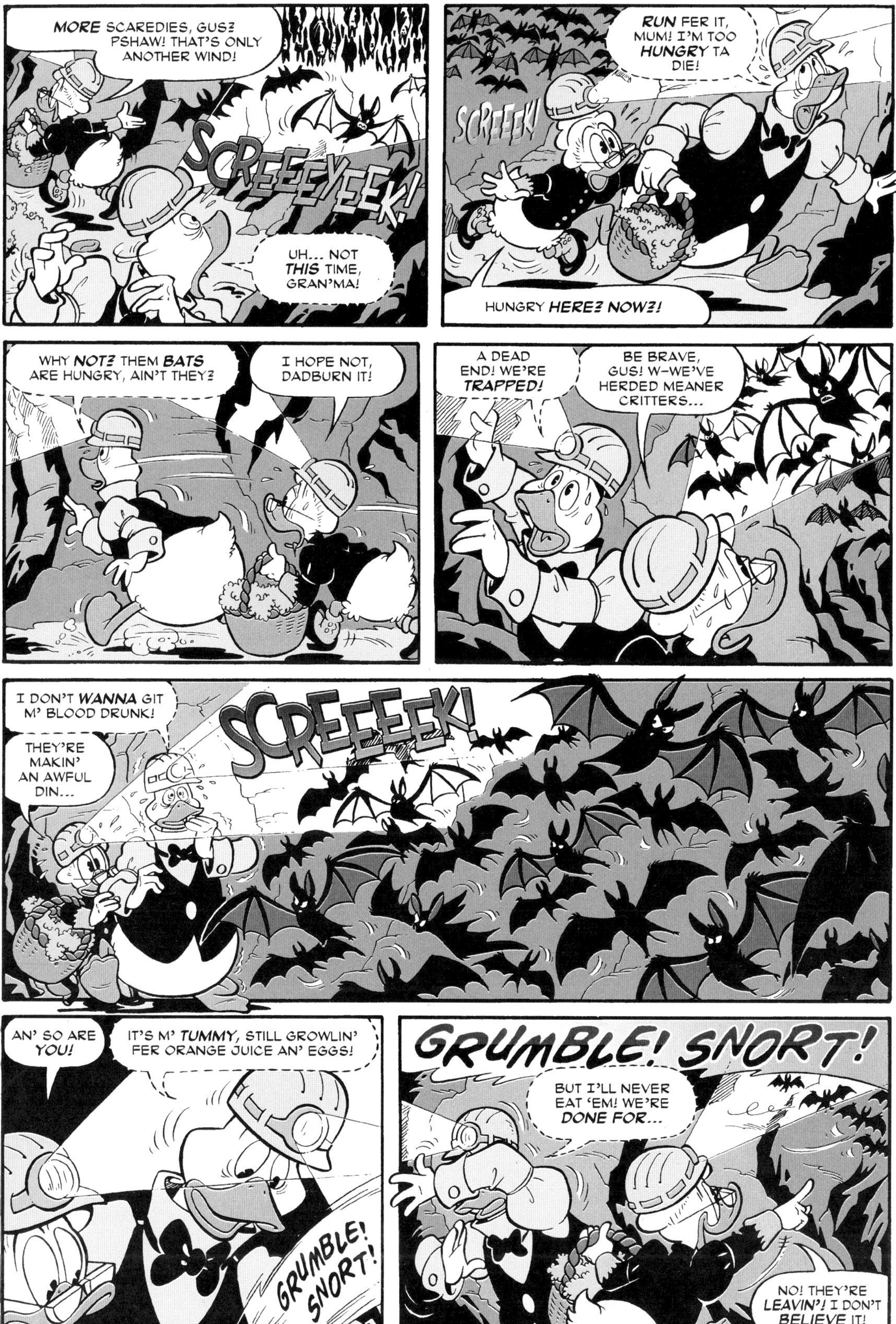
MORE SCAREDIES, GUS? PSHAW! THAT'S ONLY ANOTHER WIND!
SCREEEYEEK!
UH... NOT THIS TIME, GRAN'MA!
RUN FER IT, MUM! I'M TOO HUNGRY TA DIE!
SCREEEK!
HUNGRY HERE? NOW?!
WHY NOT? THEM BATS ARE HUNGRY, AIN'T THEY?
I HOPE NOT, DADBURN IT!
A DEAD END! WE'RE TRAPPED!
BE BRAVE, GUS! W-WE'VE HERDED MEANER CRITTERS...
I DON'T WANNA GIT M' BLOOD DRUNK!
THEY'RE MAKIN' AN AWFUL DIN...
SCREEEEK!
AN' SO ARE YOU!
IT'S M' TUMMY, STILL GROWLIN' FER ORANGE JUICE AN' EGGS!
GRUMBLE! SNORT!
GRUMBLE! SNORT!
BUT I'LL NEVER EAT 'EM! WE'RE DONE FOR...
NO! THEY'RE LEAVIN'! I DON'T BELIEVE IT!

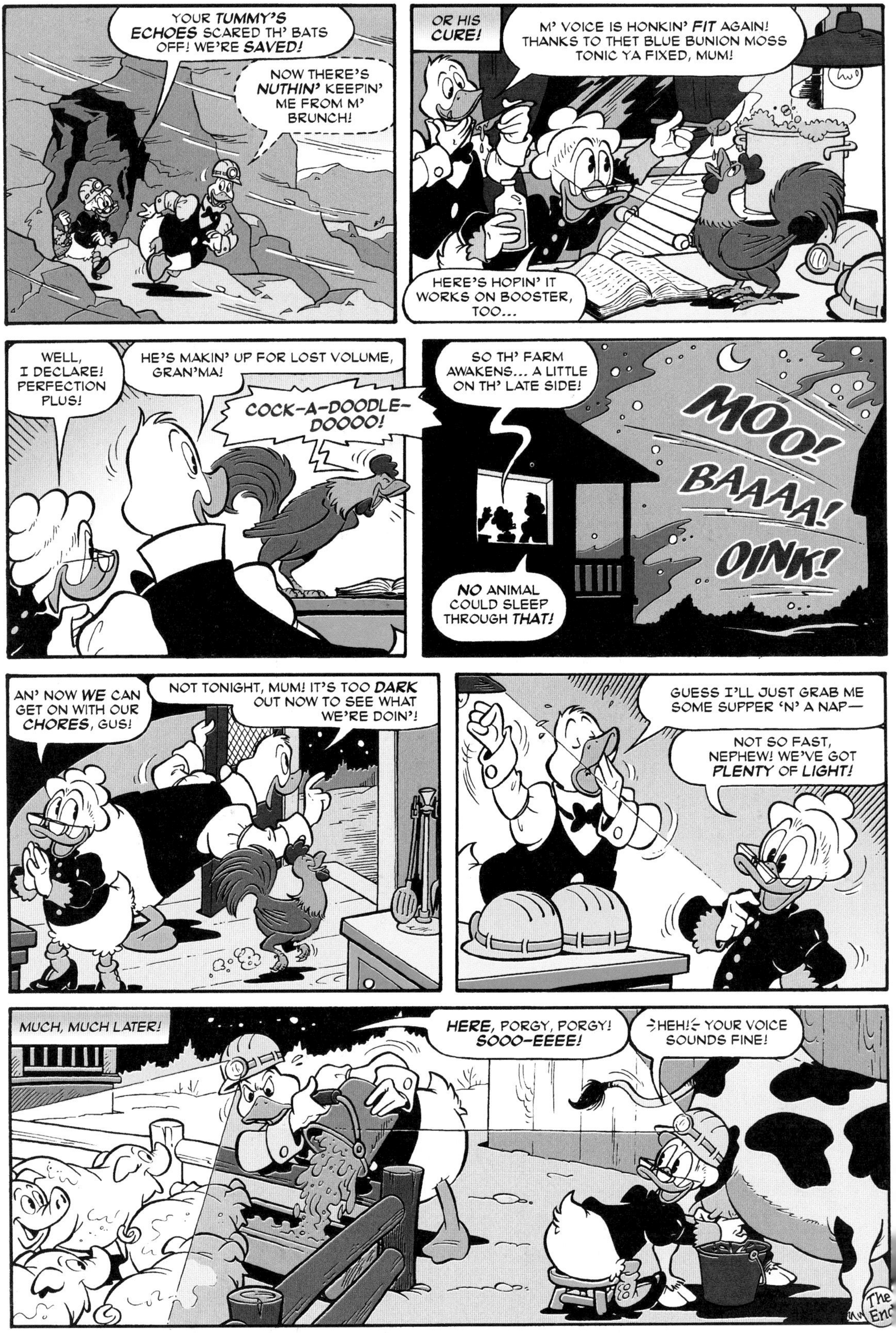
YOUR TUMMY'S ECHOES SCARED TH' BATS OFF! WE'RE SAVED!
NOW THERE'S NUTHIN' KEEPIN' ME FROM M' BRUNCH!
OR HIS CURE!
M' VOICE IS HONKIN' FIT AGAIN! THANKS TO THET BLUE BUNION MOSS TONIC YA FIXED, MUM!
HERE'S HOPIN' IT WORKS ON BOOSTER, TOO...
WELL, I DECLARE! PERFECTION PLUS!
HE'S MAKIN' UP FOR LOST VOLUME, GRAN'MA!
COCK-A-DOODLE-DOOOO!
SO TH' FARM AWAKENS... A LITTLE ON TH' LATE SIDE!
MOO!
BAAAA!
OINK!
NO ANIMAL COULD SLEEP THROUGH THAT!
AN' NOW WE CAN GET ON WITH OUR CHORES, GUS!
NOT TONIGHT, MUM! IT'S TOO DARK OUT NOW TO SEE WHAT WE'RE DOIN'!
GUESS I'LL JUST GRAB ME SOME SUPPER 'N' A NAP—
NOT SO FAST, NEPHEW! WE'VE GOT PLENTY OF LIGHT!
MUCH, MUCH LATER!
HERE, PORGY, PORGY! SOOO-EEEE!
HEH! YOUR VOICE SOUNDS FINE!
The End

Walt Disney's

DONALD DUCK

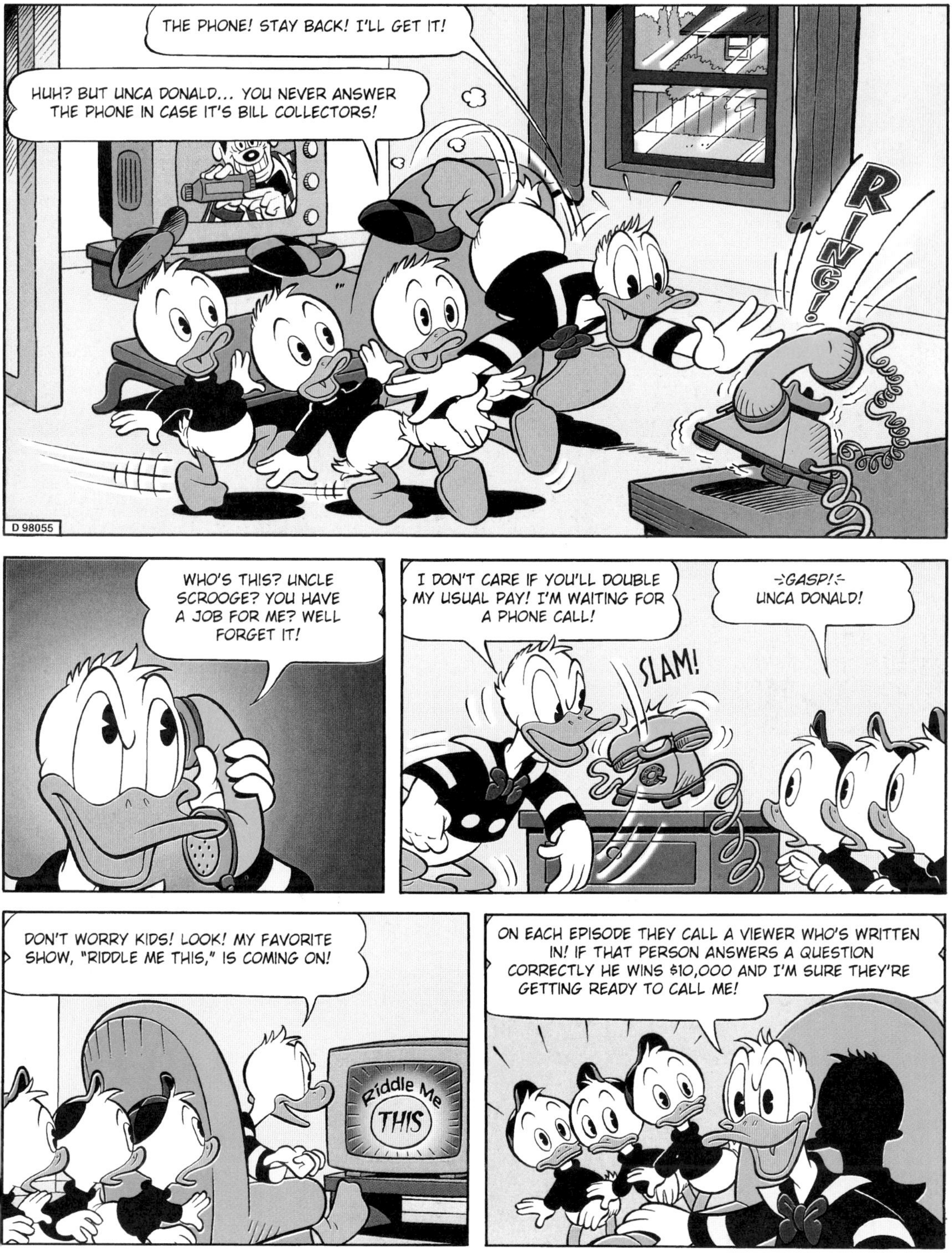
THE PHONE! STAY BACK! I'LL GET IT!
HUH? BUT UNCA DONALD... YOU NEVER ANSWER THE PHONE IN CASE IT'S BILL COLLECTORS!
RING!
D 98055
WHO'S THIS? UNCLE SCROOGE? YOU HAVE A JOB FOR ME? WELL FORGET IT!
I DON'T CARE IF YOU'LL DOUBLE MY USUAL PAY! I'M WAITING FOR A PHONE CALL!
SLAM!
GASP! UNCA DONALD!
DON'T WORRY KIDS! LOOK! MY FAVORITE SHOW, "RIDDLE ME THIS," IS COMING ON!
Riddle Me THIS
ON EACH EPISODE THEY CALL A VIEWER WHO'S WRITTEN IN! IF THAT PERSON ANSWERS A QUESTION CORRECTLY HE WINS $10,000 AND I'M SURE THEY'RE GETTING READY TO CALL ME!

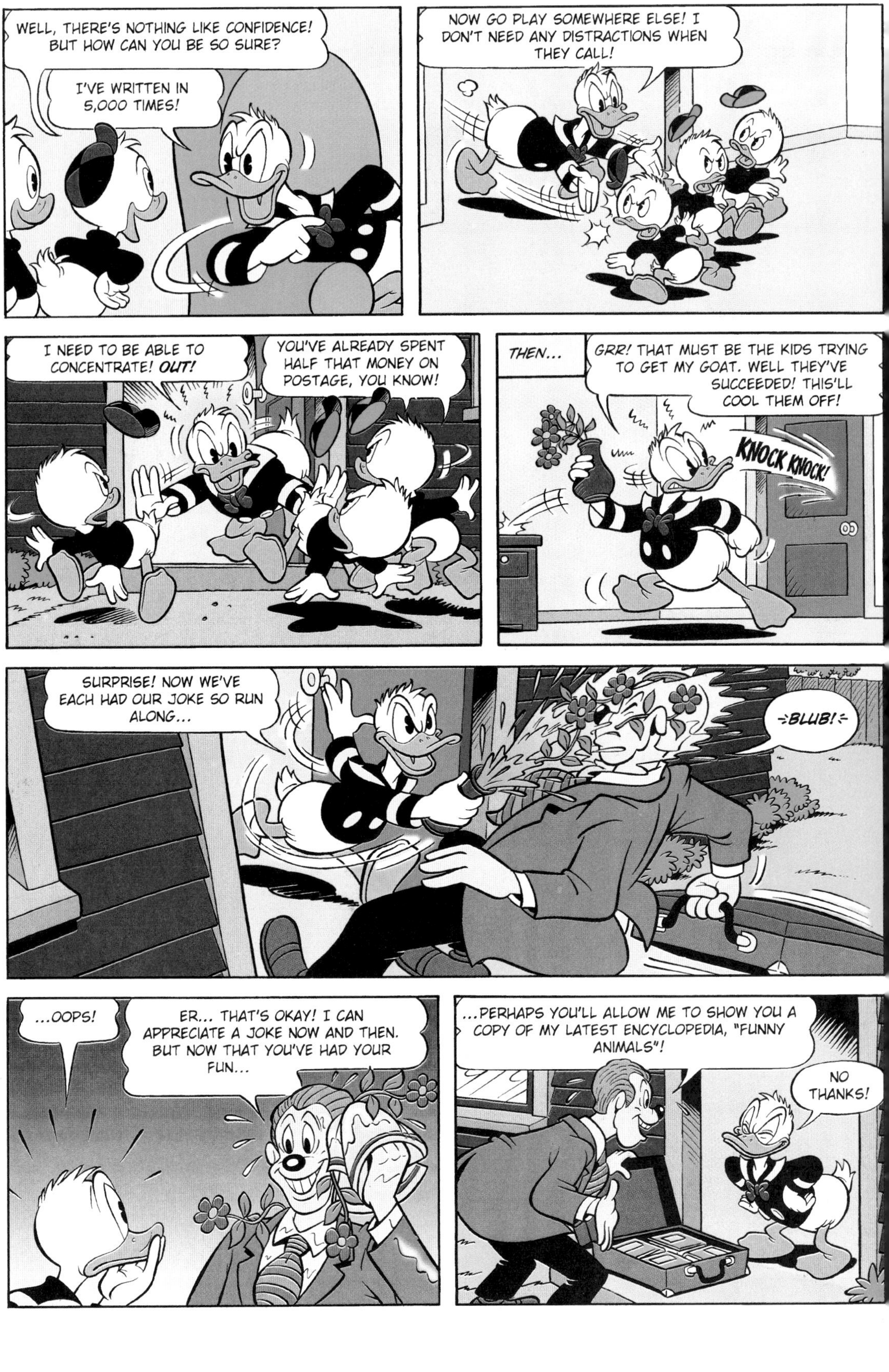
WELL, THERE'S NOTHING LIKE CONFIDENCE! BUT HOW CAN YOU BE SO SURE?
I'VE WRITTEN IN 5,000 TIMES!
NOW GO PLAY SOMEWHERE ELSE! I DON'T NEED ANY DISTRACTIONS WHEN THEY CALL!
I NEED TO BE ABLE TO CONCENTRATE! OUT!
YOU'VE ALREADY SPENT HALF THAT MONEY ON POSTAGE, YOU KNOW!
THEN...
GRR! THAT MUST BE THE KIDS TRYING TO GET MY GOAT. WELL THEY'VE SUCCEEDED! THIS'LL COOL THEM OFF!
KNOCK KNOCK!
SURPRISE! NOW WE'VE EACH HAD OUR JOKE SO RUN ALONG...
BLUB!
...OOPS!
ER... THAT'S OKAY! I CAN APPRECIATE A JOKE NOW AND THEN. BUT NOW THAT YOU'VE HAD YOUR FUN...
...PERHAPS YOU'LL ALLOW ME TO SHOW YOU A COPY OF MY LATEST ENCYCLOPEDIA, "FUNNY ANIMALS"!
NO THANKS!

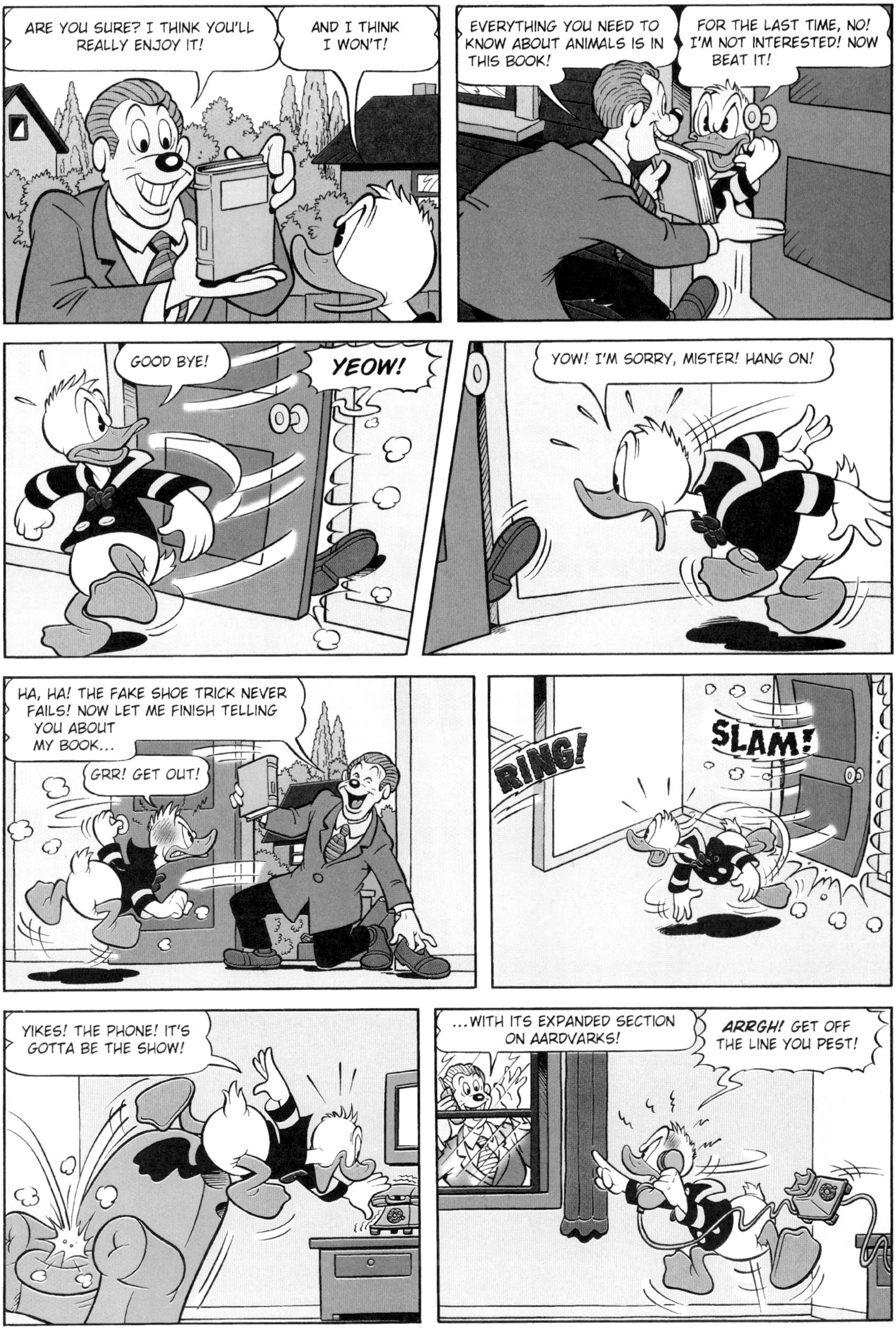
ARE YOU SURE? I THINK YOU'LL REALLY ENJOY IT!
AND I THINK I WON'T!
EVERYTHING YOU NEED TO KNOW ABOUT ANIMALS IS IN THIS BOOK!
FOR THE LAST TIME, NO! I'M NOT INTERESTED! NOW BEAT IT!
GOOD BYE!
YEOW!
YOW! I'M SORRY, MISTER! HANG ON!
HA, HA! THE FAKE SHOE TRICK NEVER FAILS! NOW LET ME FINISH TELLING YOU ABOUT MY BOOK...
GRR! GET OUT!
RING!
SLAM!
YIKES! THE PHONE! IT'S GOTTA BE THE SHOW!
...WITH ITS EXPANDED SECTION ON AARDVARKS!
ARRGH! GET OFF THE LINE YOU PEST!

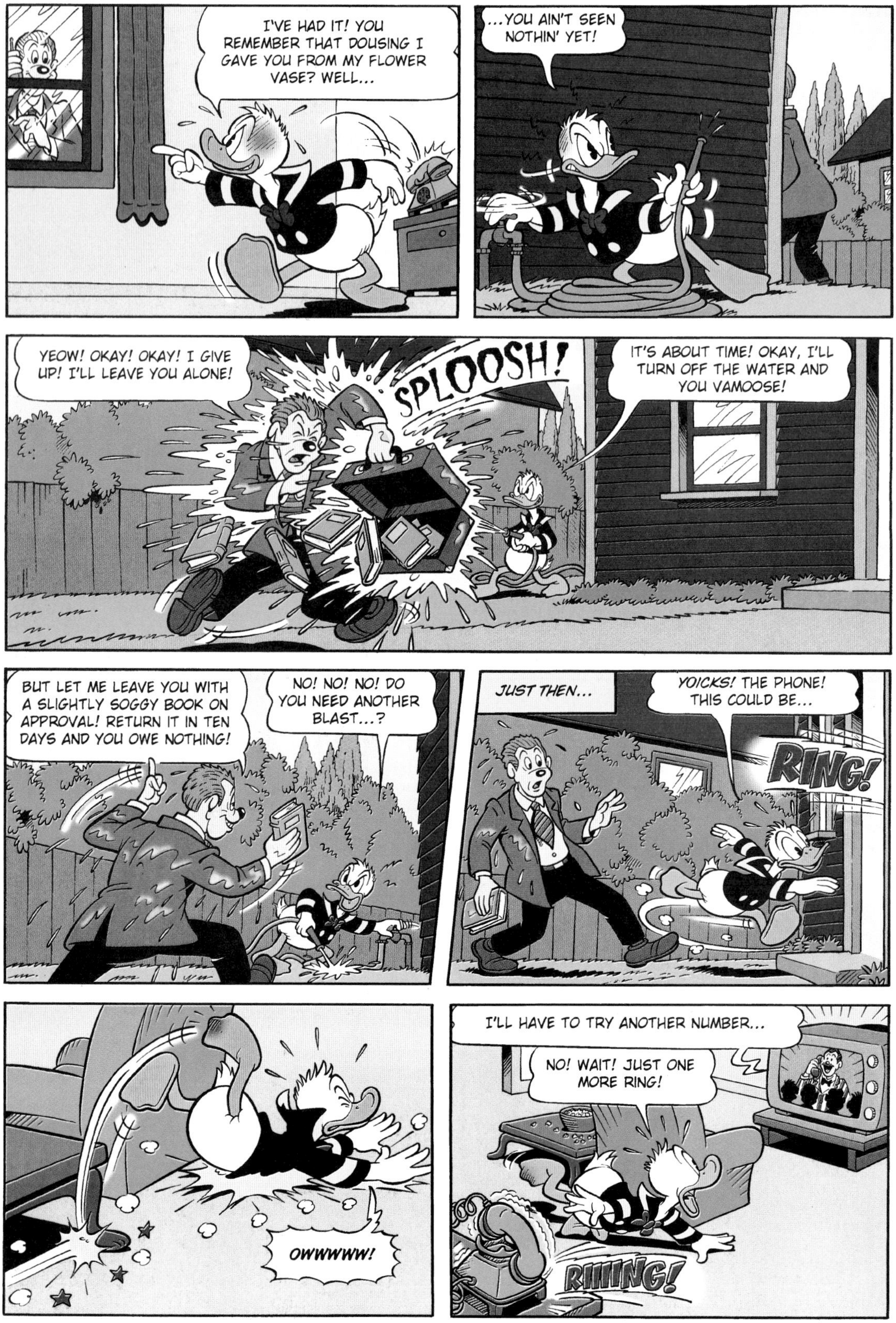
I'VE HAD IT! YOU REMEMBER THAT DOUSING I GAVE YOU FROM MY FLOWER VASE? WELL...
...YOU AIN'T SEEN NOTHIN' YET!
YEOW! OKAY! OKAY! I GIVE UP! I'LL LEAVE YOU ALONE!
SPLOOSH!
IT'S ABOUT TIME! OKAY, I'LL TURN OFF THE WATER AND YOU VAMOOSE!
BUT LET ME LEAVE YOU WITH A SLIGHTLY SOGGY BOOK ON APPROVAL! RETURN IT IN TEN DAYS AND YOU OWE NOTHING!
NO! NO! NO! DO YOU NEED ANOTHER BLAST...?
JUST THEN...
YOICKS! THE PHONE! THIS COULD BE...
RING!
OWWWWW!
I'LL HAVE TO TRY ANOTHER NUMBER...
NO! WAIT! JUST ONE MORE RING!
RIIIING!

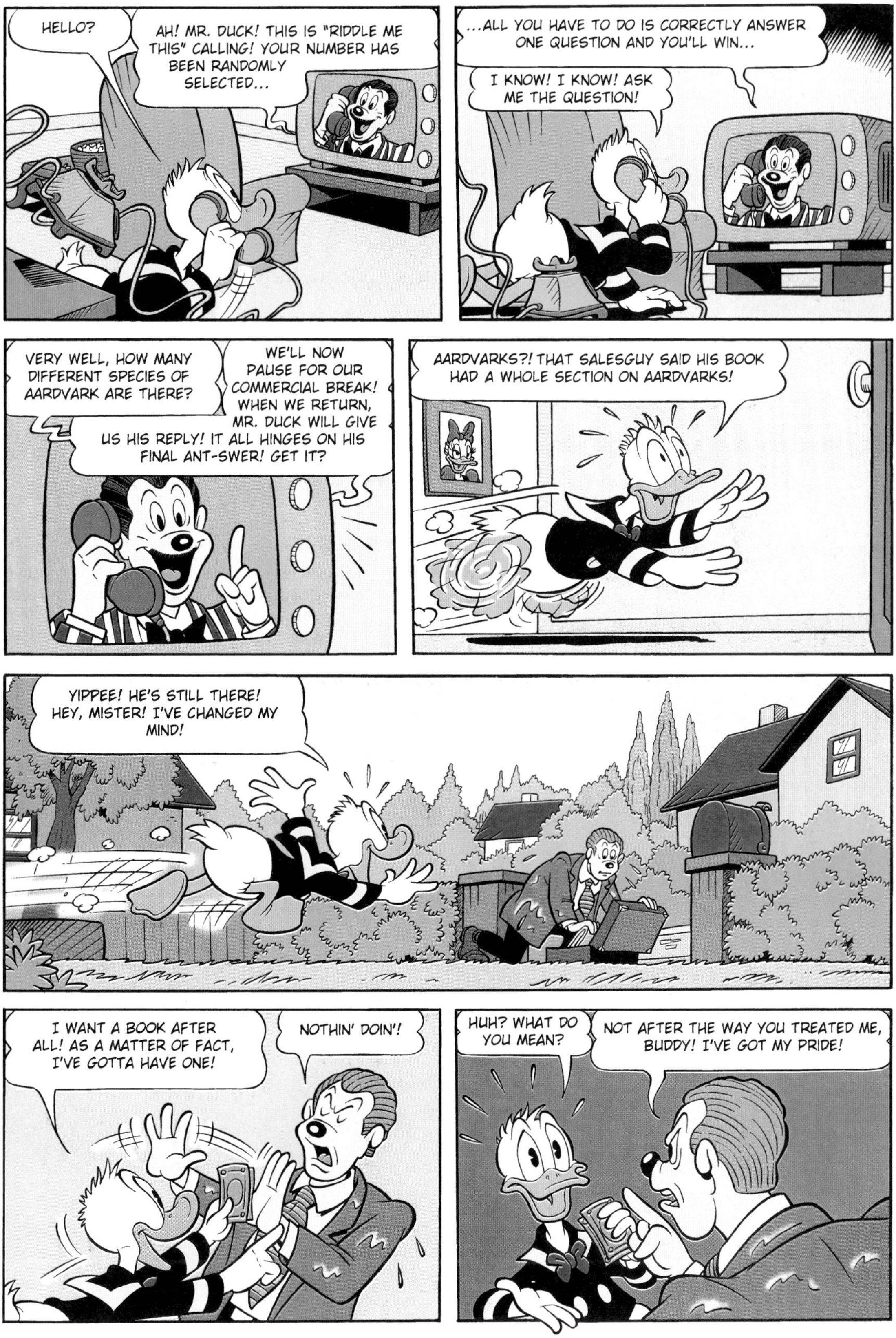
HELLO?
AH! MR. DUCK! THIS IS "RIDDLE ME THIS" CALLING! YOUR NUMBER HAS BEEN RANDOMLY SELECTED...
...ALL YOU HAVE TO DO IS CORRECTLY ANSWER ONE QUESTION AND YOU'LL WIN...
I KNOW! I KNOW! ASK ME THE QUESTION!
VERY WELL, HOW MANY DIFFERENT SPECIES OF AARDVARK ARE THERE?
WE'LL NOW PAUSE FOR OUR COMMERCIAL BREAK! WHEN WE RETURN, MR. DUCK WILL GIVE US HIS REPLY! IT ALL HINGES ON HIS FINAL ANT-SWER! GET IT?
AARDVARKS?! THAT SALESGUY SAID HIS BOOK HAD A WHOLE SECTION ON AARDVARKS!
YIPPEE! HE'S STILL THERE! HEY, MISTER! I'VE CHANGED MY MIND!
I WANT A BOOK AFTER ALL! AS A MATTER OF FACT, I'VE GOTTA HAVE ONE!
NOTHIN' DOIN'!
HUH? WHAT DO YOU MEAN?
NOT AFTER THE WAY YOU TREATED ME, BUDDY! I'VE GOT MY PRIDE!

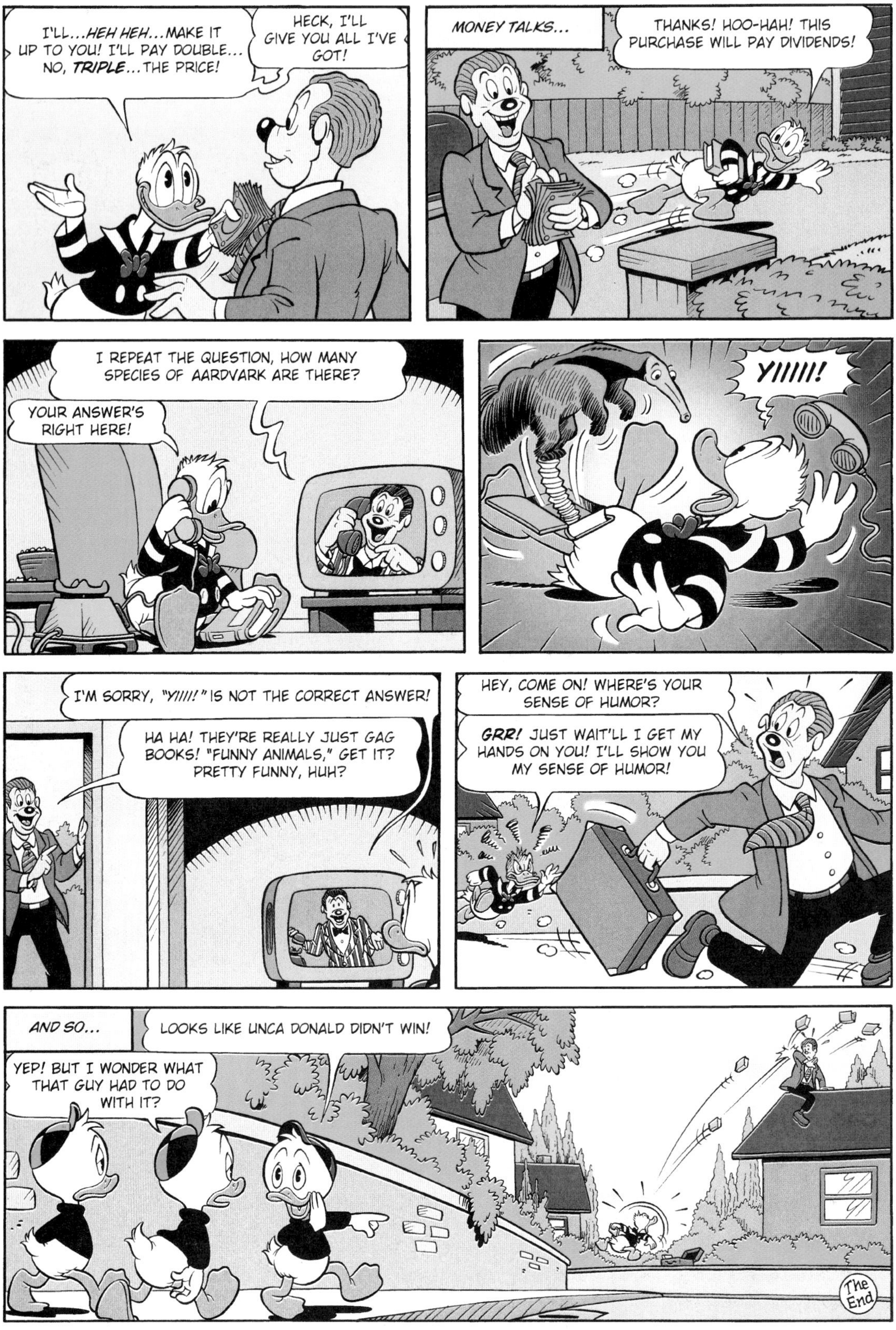
I'LL...HEH HEH...MAKE IT UP TO YOU! I'LL PAY DOUBLE... NO, TRIPLE...THE PRICE!
HECK, I'LL GIVE YOU ALL I'VE GOT!
MONEY TALKS...
THANKS! HOO-HAH! THIS PURCHASE WILL PAY DIVIDENDS!
I REPEAT THE QUESTION, HOW MANY SPECIES OF AARDVARK ARE THERE?
YOUR ANSWER'S RIGHT HERE!
YIIIII!
I'M SORRY, "YIIII!" IS NOT THE CORRECT ANSWER!
HA HA! THEY'RE REALLY JUST GAG BOOKS! "FUNNY ANIMALS," GET IT? PRETTY FUNNY, HUH?
HEY, COME ON! WHERE'S YOUR SENSE OF HUMOR?
GRR! JUST WAIT'LL I GET MY HANDS ON YOU! I'LL SHOW YOU MY SENSE OF HUMOR!
AND SO...
LOOKS LIKE UNCA DONALD DIDN'T WIN!
YEP! BUT I WONDER WHAT THAT GUY HAD TO DO WITH IT?
The End

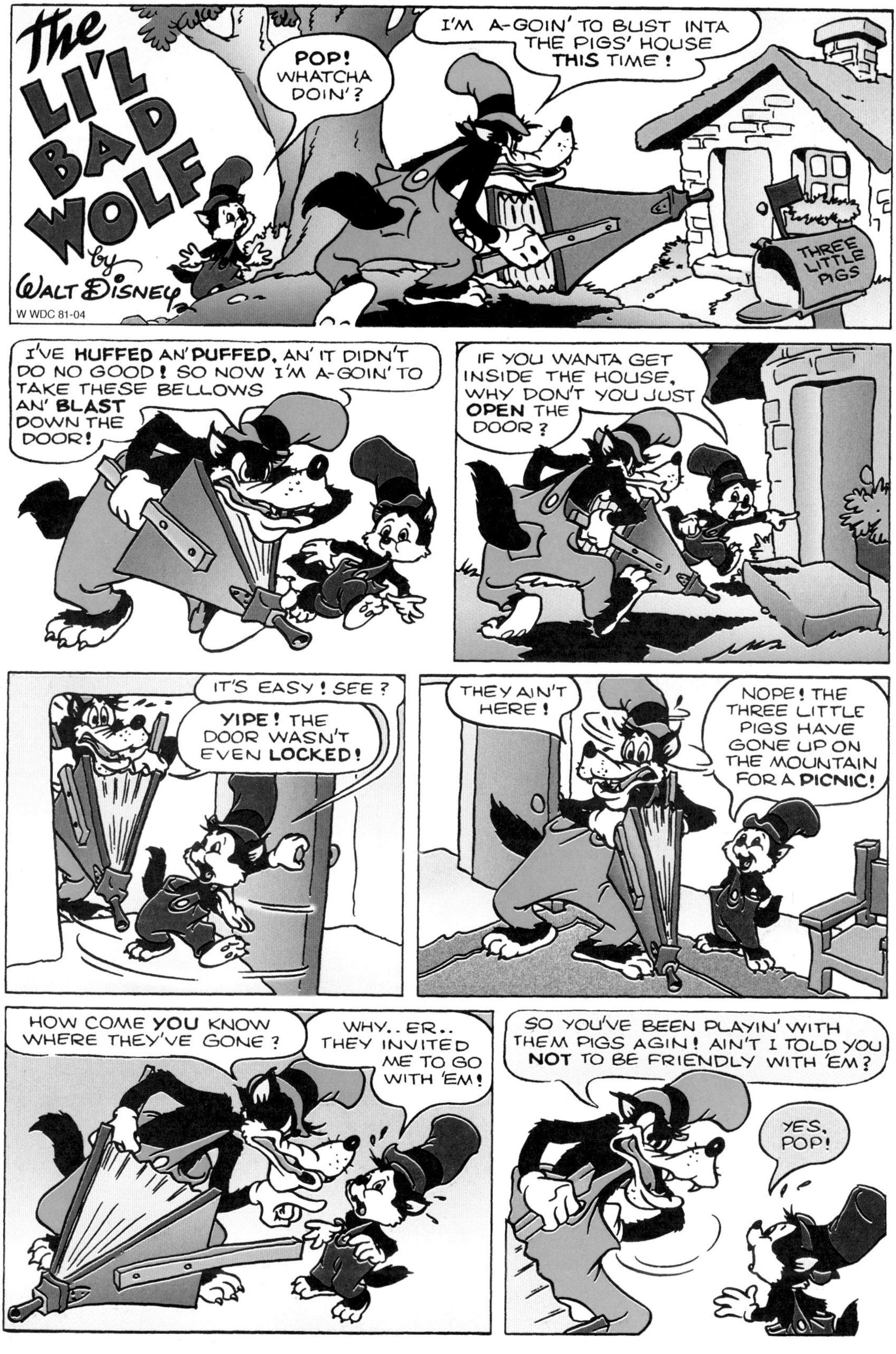

the LI'L BAD WOLF
by WALT DISNEY
W WDC 81-04
POP! WHATCHA DOIN'?
I'M A-GOIN' TO BUST INTA THE PIGS' HOUSE **THIS** TIME!
THREE LITTLE PIGS
I'VE **HUFFED** AN' **PUFFED**, AN' IT DIDN'T DO NO GOOD! SO NOW I'M A-GOIN' TO TAKE THESE BELLOWS AN' **BLAST** DOWN THE DOOR!
IF YOU WANTA GET INSIDE THE HOUSE, WHY DON'T YOU JUST **OPEN** THE DOOR?
IT'S EASY! SEE?
YIPE! THE DOOR WASN'T EVEN **LOCKED**!
THEY AIN'T HERE!
NOPE! THE THREE LITTLE PIGS HAVE GONE UP ON THE MOUNTAIN FOR A **PICNIC**!
HOW COME **YOU** KNOW WHERE THEY'VE GONE?
WHY.. ER.. THEY INVITED ME TO GO WITH 'EM!
SO YOU'VE BEEN PLAYIN' WITH THEM PIGS AGIN! AIN'T I TOLD YOU **NOT** TO BE FRIENDLY WITH 'EM?
YES, POP!

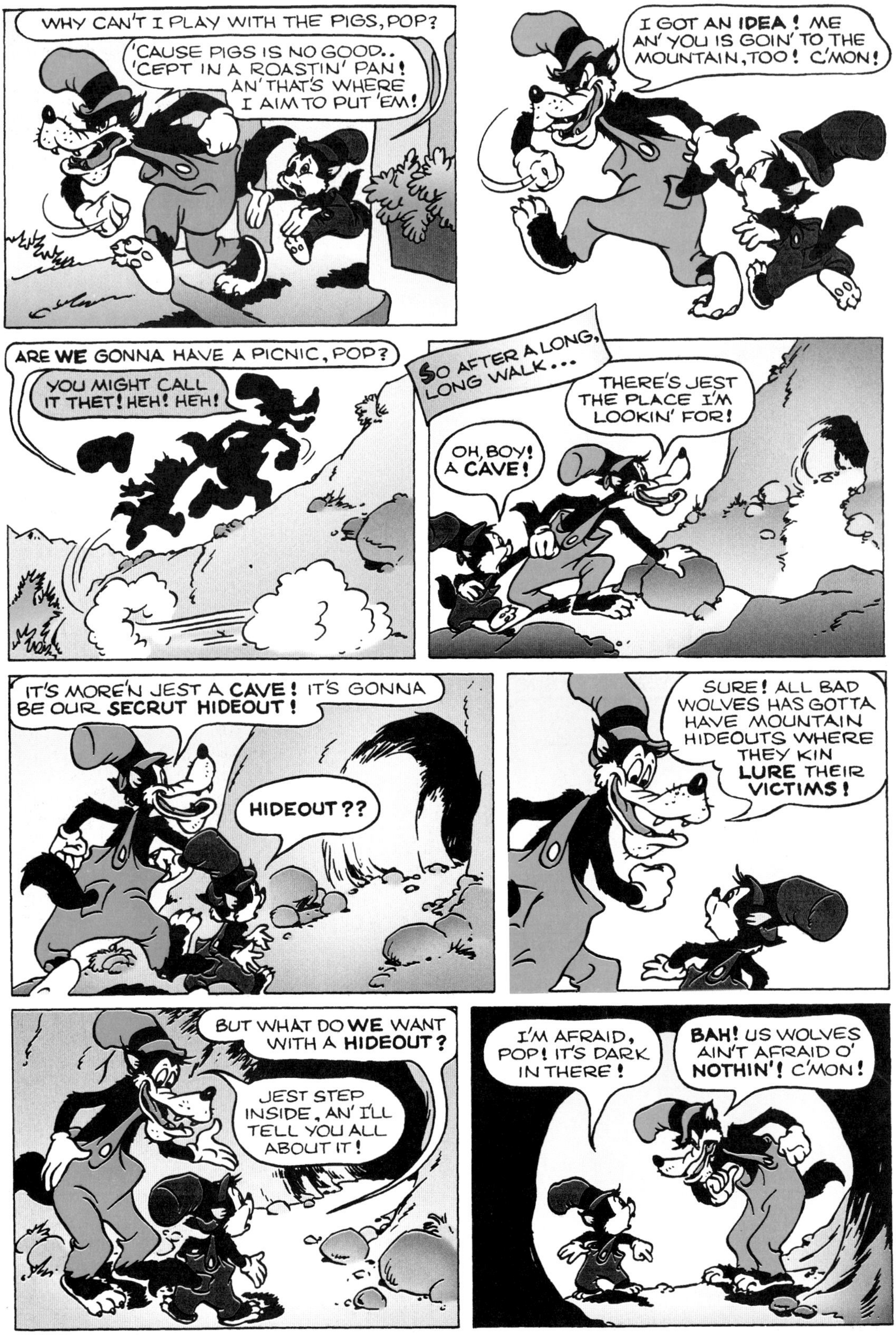
WHY CAN'T I PLAY WITH THE PIGS, POP?
'CAUSE PIGS IS NO GOOD.. 'CEPT IN A ROASTIN' PAN! AN' THAT'S WHERE I AIM TO PUT 'EM!
I GOT AN IDEA! ME AN' YOU IS GOIN' TO THE MOUNTAIN, TOO! C'MON!
ARE WE GONNA HAVE A PICNIC, POP?
YOU MIGHT CALL IT THET! HEH! HEH!
SO AFTER A LONG, LONG WALK...
THERE'S JEST THE PLACE I'M LOOKIN' FOR!
OH, BOY! A CAVE!
IT'S MORE'N JEST A CAVE! IT'S GONNA BE OUR SECRUT HIDEOUT!
HIDEOUT??
SURE! ALL BAD WOLVES HAS GOTTA HAVE MOUNTAIN HIDEOUTS WHERE THEY KIN LURE THEIR VICTIMS!
BUT WHAT DO WE WANT WITH A HIDEOUT?
JEST STEP INSIDE, AN' I'LL TELL YOU ALL ABOUT IT!
I'M AFRAID, POP! IT'S DARK IN THERE!
BAH! US WOLVES AIN'T AFRAID O' NOTHIN'! C'MON!

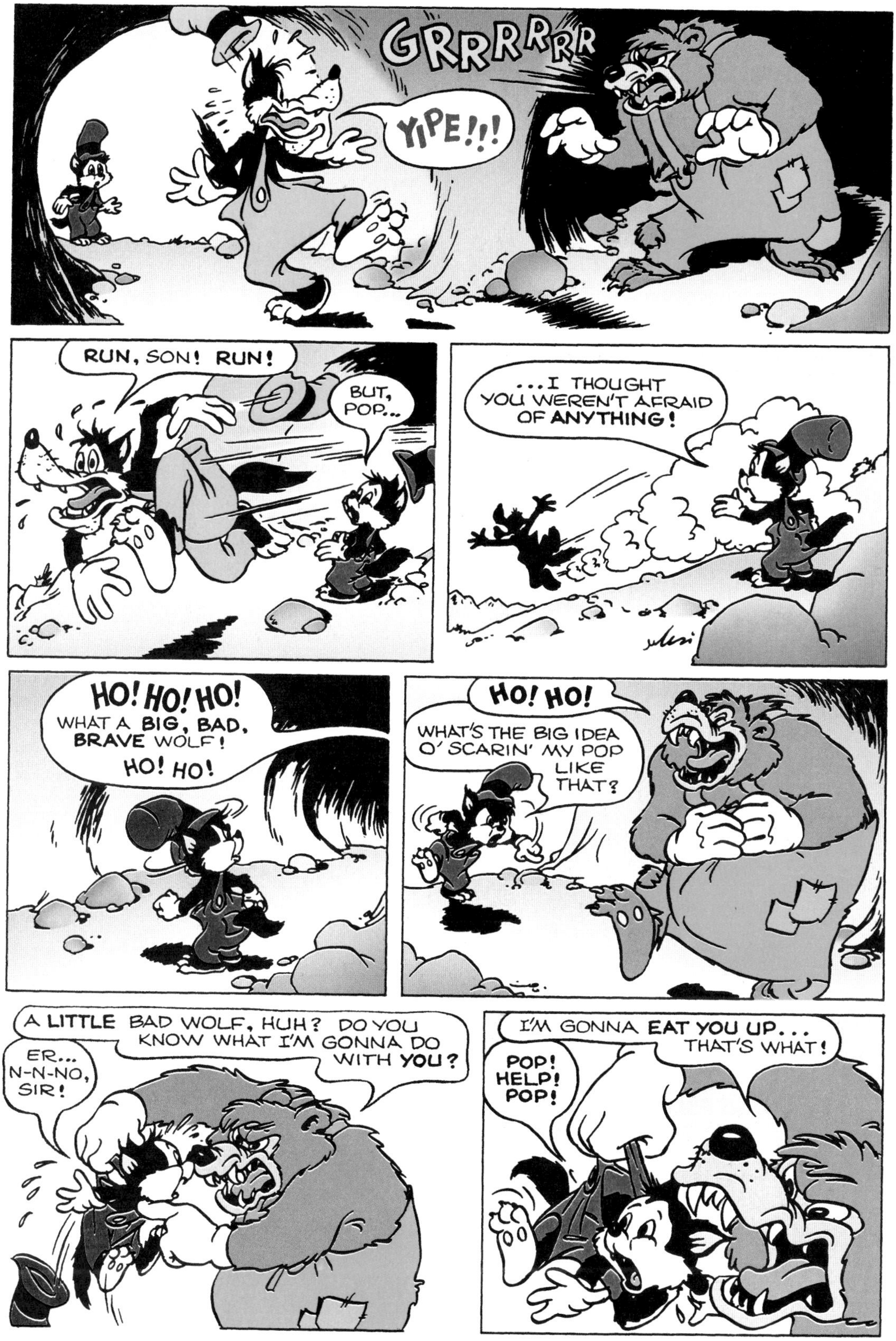
GRRRRRR
YIPE!!!
RUN, SON! RUN!
BUT, POP...
...I THOUGHT YOU WEREN'T AFRAID OF ANYTHING!
HO! HO! HO! WHAT A BIG, BAD, BRAVE WOLF! HO! HO!
HO! HO!
WHAT'S THE BIG IDEA O' SCARIN' MY POP LIKE THAT?
A LITTLE BAD WOLF, HUH? DO YOU KNOW WHAT I'M GONNA DO WITH YOU?
ER... N-N-NO, SIR!
I'M GONNA EAT YOU UP... THAT'S WHAT!
POP! HELP! POP!

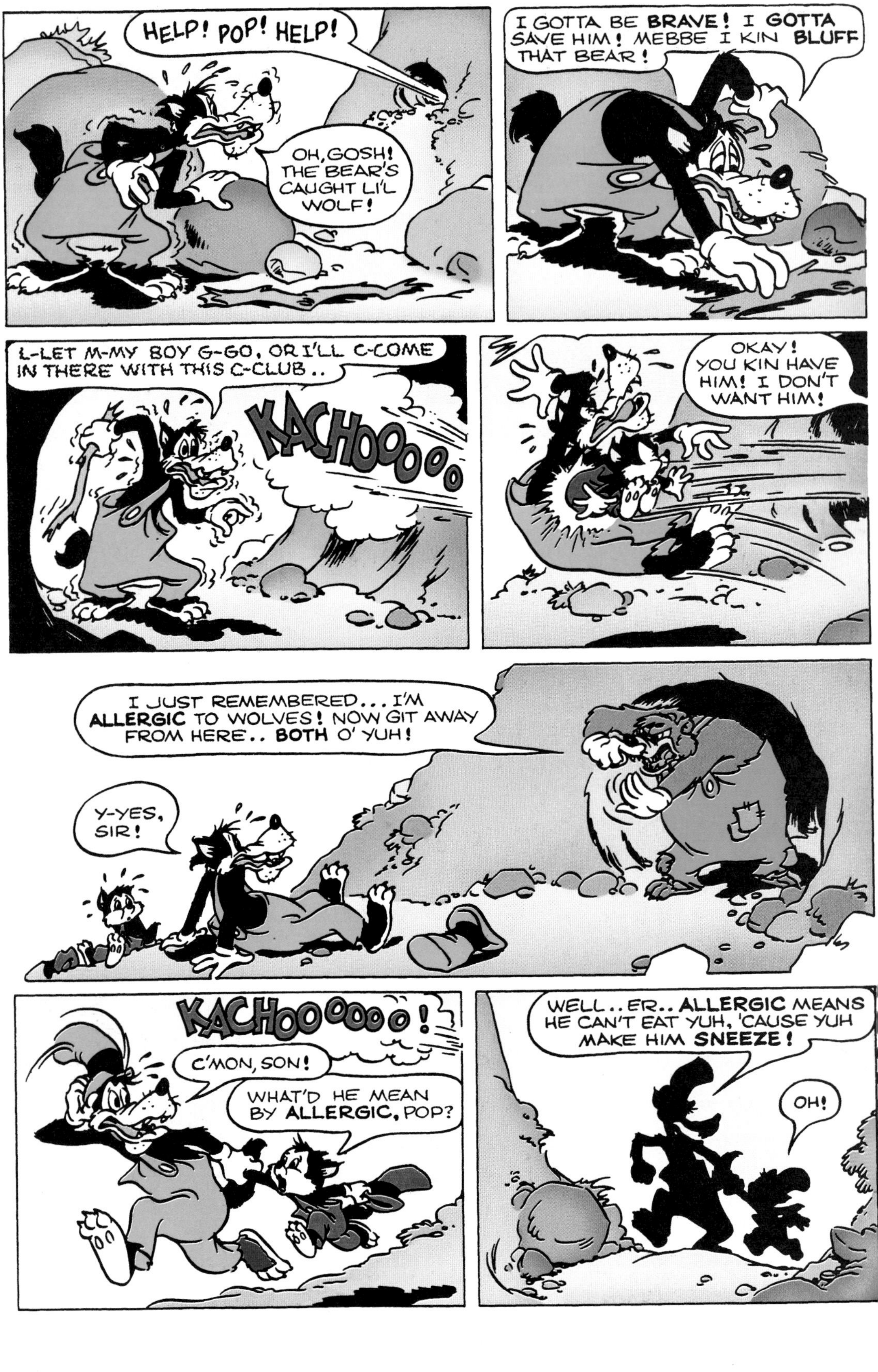
HELP! POP! HELP!
OH, GOSH! THE BEAR'S CAUGHT LI'L WOLF!
I GOTTA BE BRAVE! I GOTTA SAVE HIM! MEBBE I KIN BLUFF THAT BEAR!
L-LET M-MY BOY G-GO, OR I'LL C-COME IN THERE WITH THIS C-CLUB..
KACHOOOOOO
OKAY! YOU KIN HAVE HIM! I DON'T WANT HIM!
I JUST REMEMBERED... I'M ALLERGIC TO WOLVES! NOW GIT AWAY FROM HERE.. BOTH O' YUH!
Y-YES, SIR!
KACHOOOOOOO!
C'MON, SON!
WHAT'D HE MEAN BY ALLERGIC, POP?
WELL..ER.. ALLERGIC MEANS HE CAN'T EAT YUH, 'CAUSE YUH MAKE HIM SNEEZE!
OH!

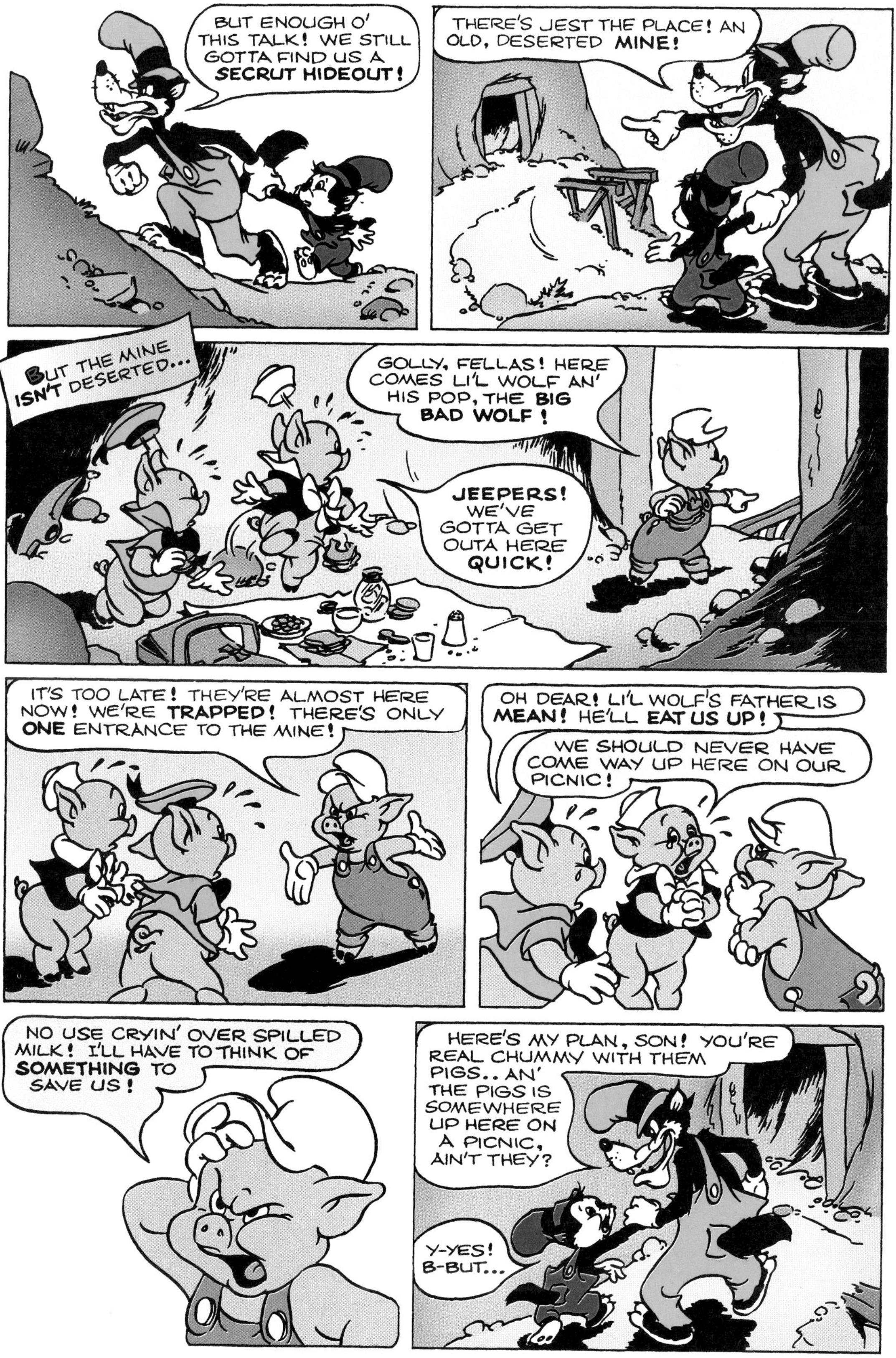

BUT ENOUGH O' THIS TALK! WE STILL GOTTA FIND US A **SECRUT HIDEOUT**!
THERE'S JEST THE PLACE! AN OLD, DESERTED **MINE**!
BUT THE MINE **ISN'T** DESERTED...
GOLLY, FELLAS! HERE COMES LI'L WOLF AN' HIS POP, THE **BIG BAD WOLF**!
JEEPERS! WE'VE GOTTA GET OUTA HERE **QUICK!**
IT'S TOO LATE! THEY'RE ALMOST HERE NOW! WE'RE **TRAPPED!** THERE'S ONLY **ONE** ENTRANCE TO THE MINE!
OH DEAR! LI'L WOLF'S FATHER IS **MEAN!** HE'LL **EAT US UP!**
WE SHOULD NEVER HAVE COME WAY UP HERE ON OUR PICNIC!
NO USE CRYIN' OVER SPILLED MILK! I'LL HAVE TO THINK OF **SOMETHING** TO SAVE US!
HERE'S MY PLAN, SON! YOU'RE REAL CHUMMY WITH THEM PIGS.. AN' THE PIGS IS SOMEWHERE UP HERE ON A PICNIC, AIN'T THEY?
Y-YES! B-BUT...

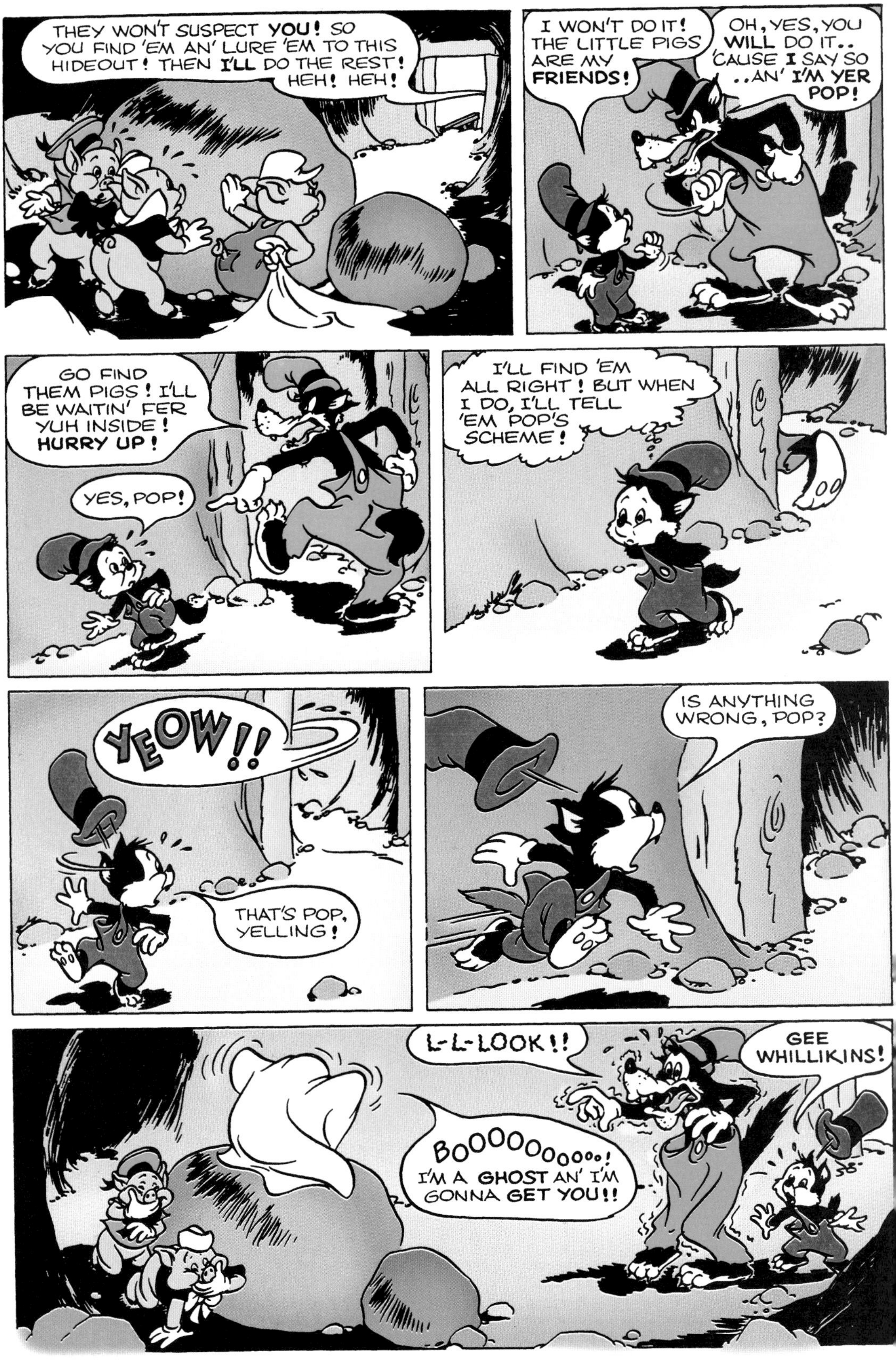

THEY WON'T SUSPECT YOU! SO YOU FIND 'EM AN' LURE 'EM TO THIS HIDEOUT! THEN I'LL DO THE REST! HEH! HEH!
I WON'T DO IT! THE LITTLE PIGS ARE MY FRIENDS!
OH, YES, YOU WILL DO IT.. 'CAUSE I SAY SO ..AN' I'M YER POP!
GO FIND THEM PIGS! I'LL BE WAITIN' FER YUH INSIDE! HURRY UP!
YES, POP!
I'LL FIND 'EM ALL RIGHT! BUT WHEN I DO, I'LL TELL 'EM POP'S SCHEME!
YEOW!!
THAT'S POP, YELLING!
IS ANYTHING WRONG, POP?
L-L-LOOK!!
GEE WHILLIKINS!
BOOOOOOooooo! I'M A GHOST AN' I'M GONNA GET YOU!!

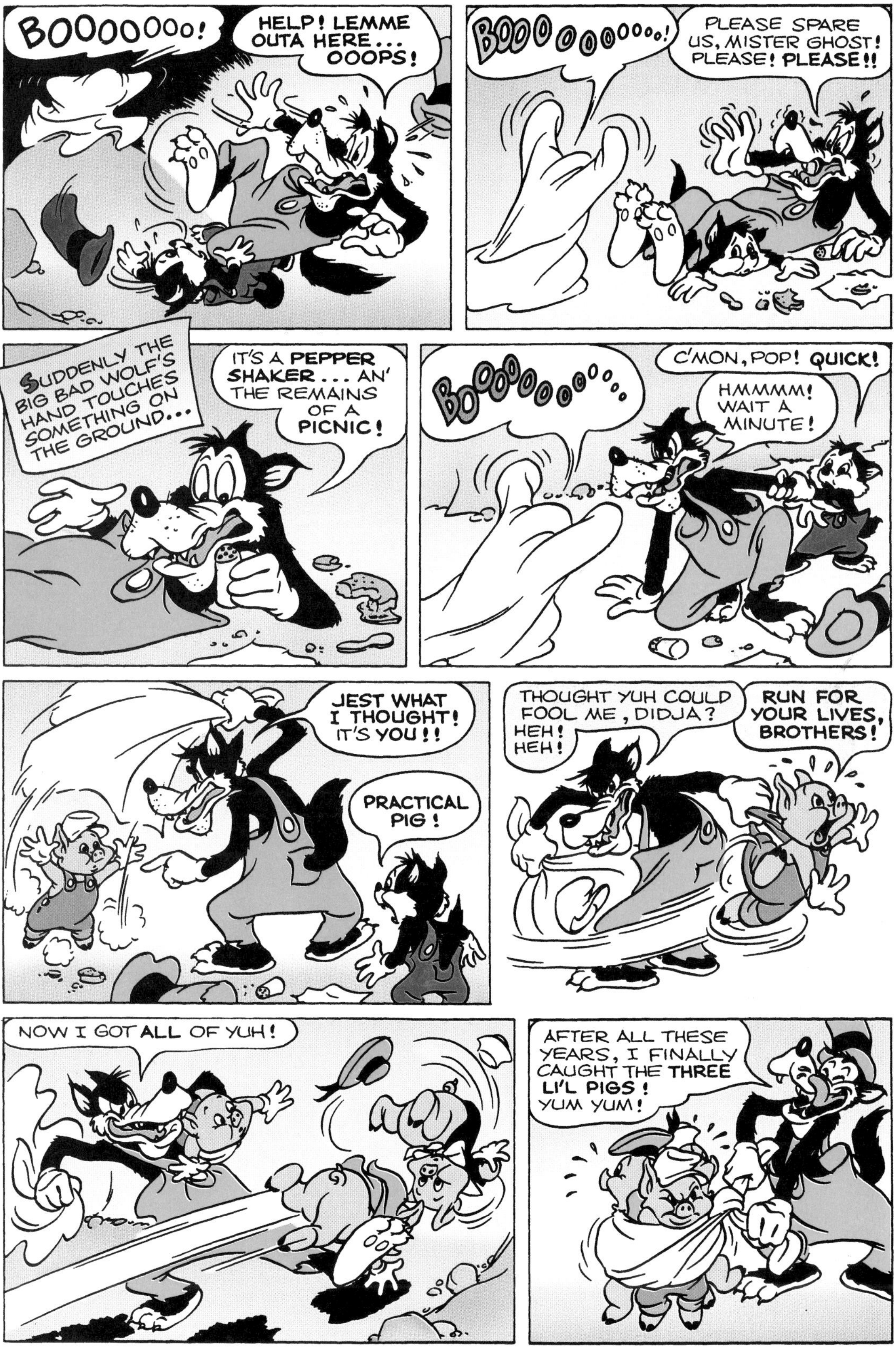

BOOOOOOo!
HELP! LEMME OUTA HERE... OOOPS!
BOOOOOOOOo!
PLEASE SPARE US, MISTER GHOST! PLEASE! PLEASE!!
SUDDENLY THE BIG BAD WOLF'S HAND TOUCHES SOMETHING ON THE GROUND...
IT'S A PEPPER SHAKER... AN' THE REMAINS OF A PICNIC!
BOOOOOOOOOOOO
C'MON, POP! QUICK!
HMMMM! WAIT A MINUTE!
JEST WHAT I THOUGHT! IT'S YOU!!
PRACTICAL PIG!
THOUGHT YUH COULD FOOL ME, DIDJA? HEH! HEH!
RUN FOR YOUR LIVES, BROTHERS!
NOW I GOT ALL OF YUH!
AFTER ALL THESE YEARS, I FINALLY CAUGHT THE THREE LI'L PIGS! YUM YUM!

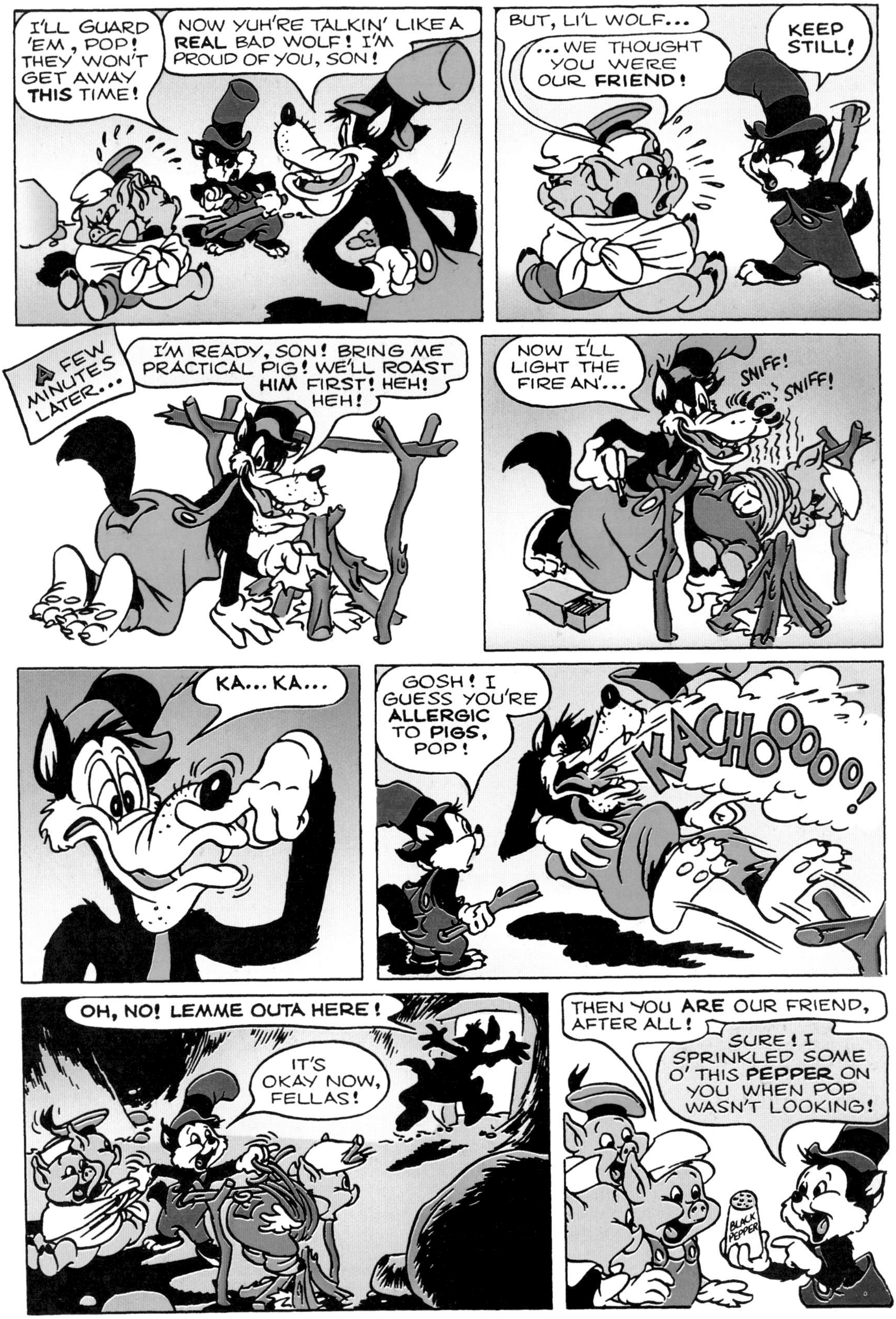
I'LL GUARD 'EM, POP! THEY WON'T GET AWAY **THIS** TIME!
NOW YUH'RE TALKIN' LIKE A **REAL** BAD WOLF! I'M PROUD OF YOU, SON!
BUT, LI'L WOLF...
...WE THOUGHT YOU WERE OUR **FRIEND**!
KEEP STILL!
A FEW MINUTES LATER...
I'M READY, SON! BRING ME PRACTICAL PIG! WE'LL ROAST **HIM** FIRST! HEH! HEH!
NOW I'LL LIGHT THE FIRE AN'...
SNIFF! SNIFF!
KA... KA...
GOSH! I GUESS YOU'RE **ALLERGIC** TO **PIGS**, POP!
KACHOOOOOO!
OH, NO! LEMME OUTA HERE!
IT'S OKAY NOW, FELLAS!
THEN YOU **ARE** OUR FRIEND, AFTER ALL!
SURE! I SPRINKLED SOME O' THIS **PEPPER** ON YOU WHEN POP WASN'T LOOKING!
BLACK PEPPER

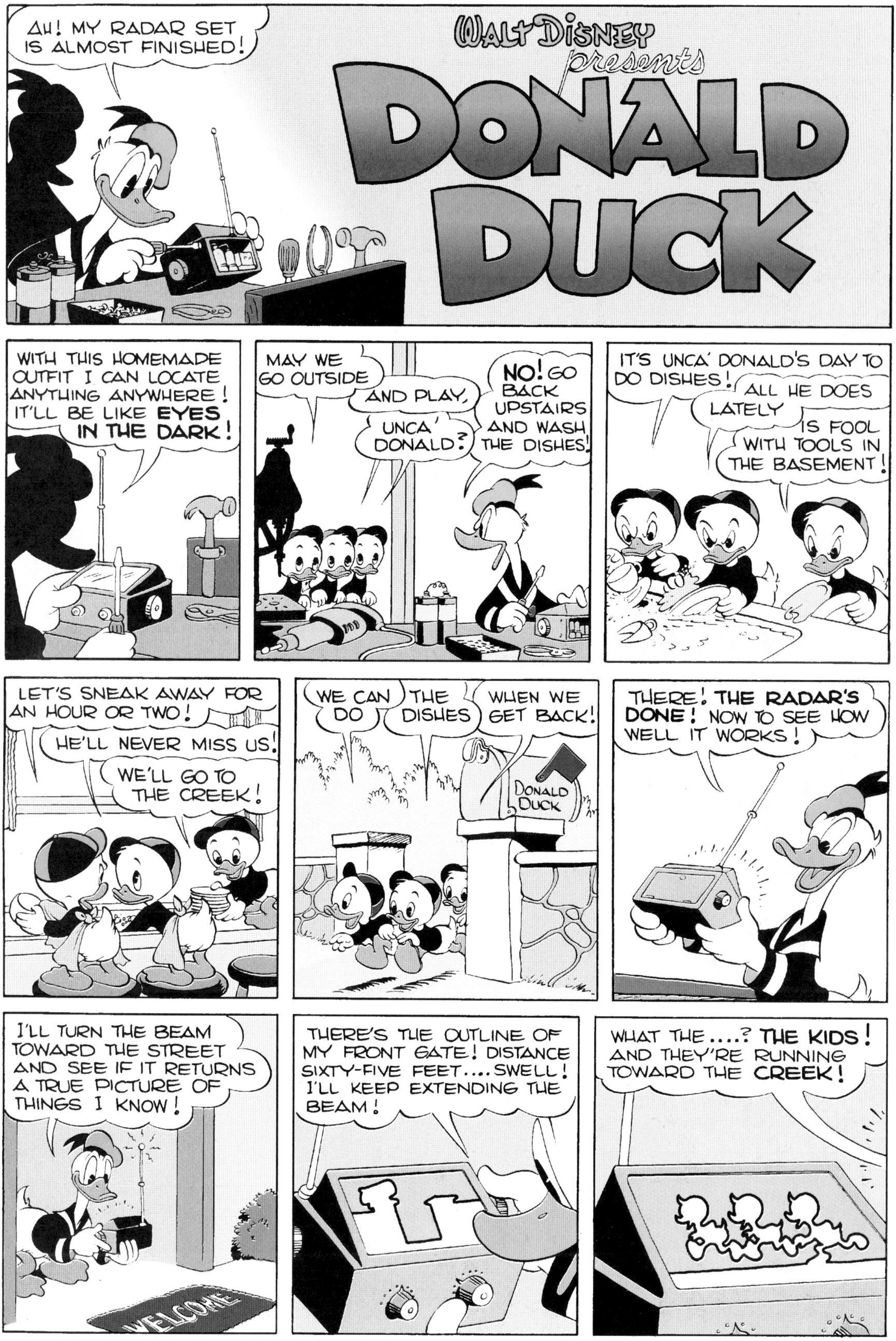
AH! MY RADAR SET IS ALMOST FINISHED!
WALT DISNEY presents
DONALD DUCK
WITH THIS HOMEMADE OUTFIT I CAN LOCATE ANYTHING ANYWHERE! IT'LL BE LIKE EYES IN THE DARK!
MAY WE GO OUTSIDE
AND PLAY,
UNCA' DONALD?
NO! GO BACK UPSTAIRS AND WASH THE DISHES!
IT'S UNCA' DONALD'S DAY TO DO DISHES!
ALL HE DOES LATELY
IS FOOL WITH TOOLS IN THE BASEMENT!
LET'S SNEAK AWAY FOR AN HOUR OR TWO!
HE'LL NEVER MISS US!
WE'LL GO TO THE CREEK!
WE CAN DO
THE DISHES
WHEN WE GET BACK!
DONALD DUCK
THERE! THE RADAR'S DONE! NOW TO SEE HOW WELL IT WORKS!
I'LL TURN THE BEAM TOWARD THE STREET AND SEE IF IT RETURNS A TRUE PICTURE OF THINGS I KNOW!
WELCOME
THERE'S THE OUTLINE OF MY FRONT GATE! DISTANCE SIXTY-FIVE FEET.... SWELL! I'LL KEEP EXTENDING THE BEAM!
WHAT THE....? THE KIDS! AND THEY'RE RUNNING TOWARD THE CREEK!

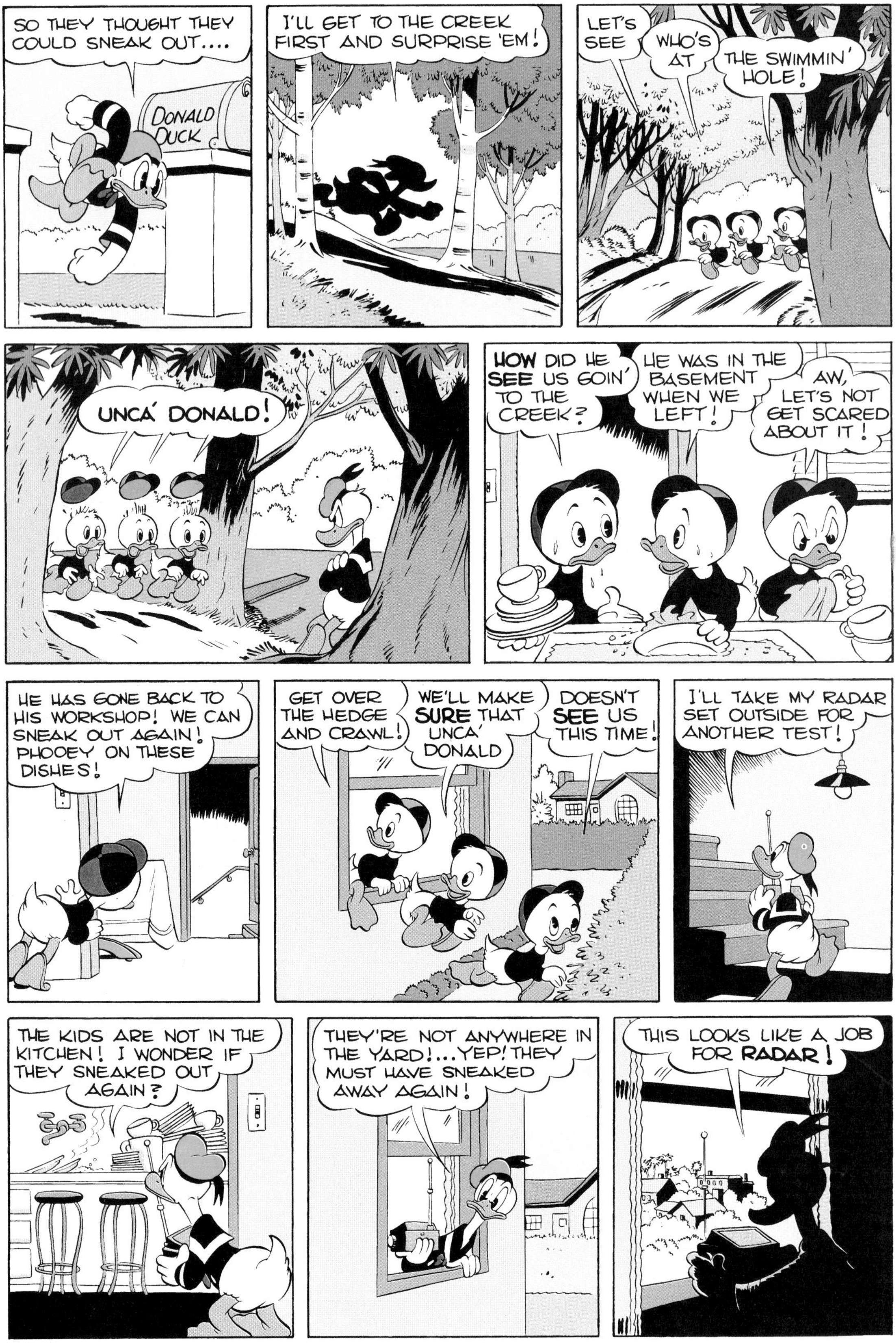
SO THEY THOUGHT THEY COULD SNEAK OUT....
DONALD DUCK
I'LL GET TO THE CREEK FIRST AND SURPRISE 'EM!
LET'S SEE
WHO'S AT
THE SWIMMIN' HOLE!
UNCA' DONALD!
HOW DID HE SEE US GOIN' TO THE CREEK?
HE WAS IN THE BASEMENT WHEN WE LEFT!
AW, LET'S NOT GET SCARED ABOUT IT!
HE HAS GONE BACK TO HIS WORKSHOP! WE CAN SNEAK OUT AGAIN! PHOOEY ON THESE DISHES!
GET OVER THE HEDGE AND CRAWL!
WE'LL MAKE SURE THAT UNCA' DONALD
DOESN'T SEE US THIS TIME!
I'LL TAKE MY RADAR SET OUTSIDE FOR ANOTHER TEST!
THE KIDS ARE NOT IN THE KITCHEN! I WONDER IF THEY SNEAKED OUT AGAIN?
THEY'RE NOT ANYWHERE IN THE YARD!... YEP! THEY MUST HAVE SNEAKED AWAY AGAIN!
THIS LOOKS LIKE A JOB FOR RADAR!

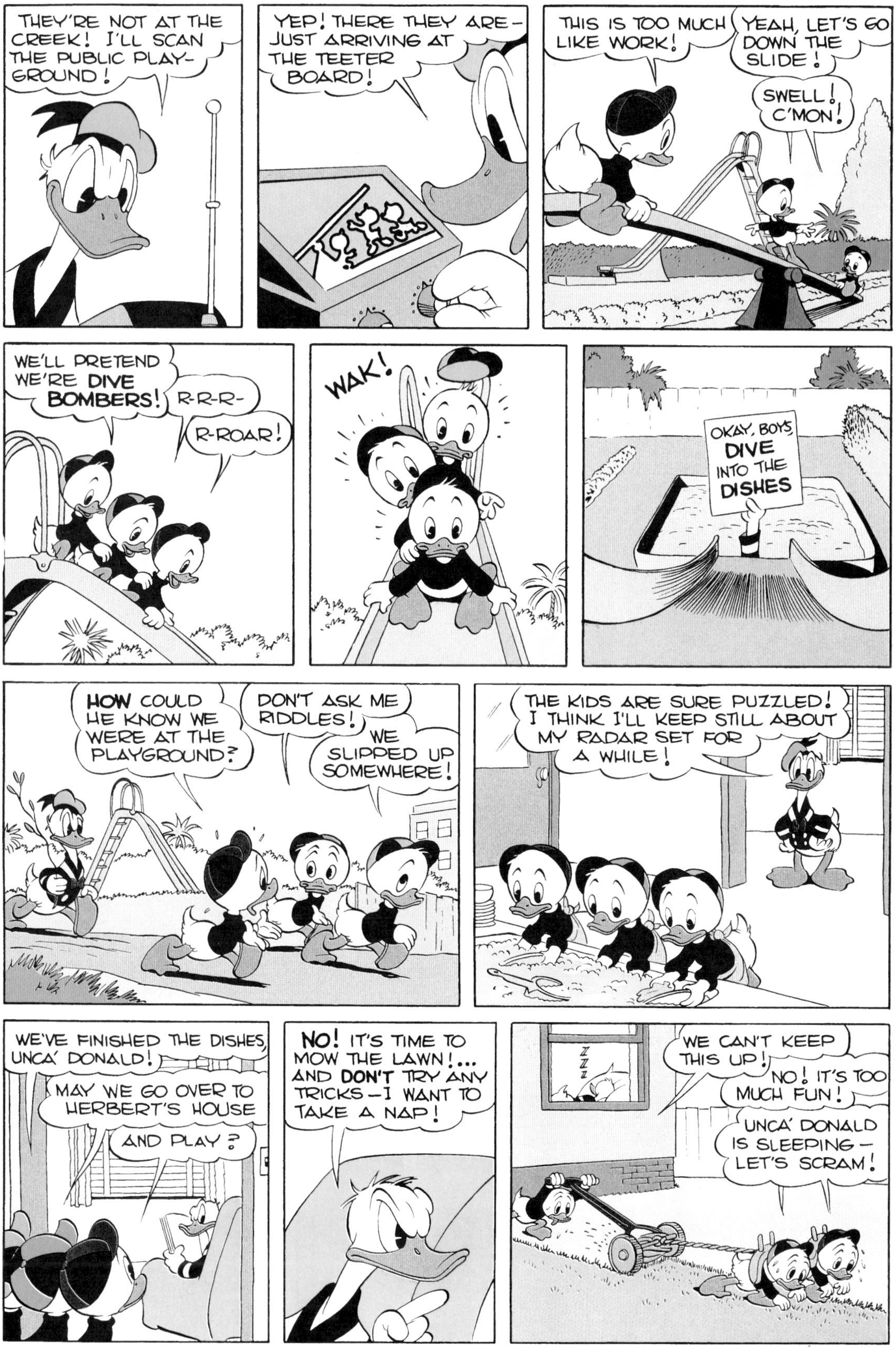
THEY'RE NOT AT THE CREEK! I'LL SCAN THE PUBLIC PLAYGROUND!
YEP! THERE THEY ARE— JUST ARRIVING AT THE TEETER BOARD!
THIS IS TOO MUCH LIKE WORK!
YEAH, LET'S GO DOWN THE SLIDE!
SWELL! C'MON!
WE'LL PRETEND WE'RE DIVE BOMBERS!
R-R-R-
R-ROAR!
WAK!
OKAY, BOYS, DIVE INTO THE DISHES
HOW COULD HE KNOW WE WERE AT THE PLAYGROUND?
DON'T ASK ME RIDDLES!
WE SLIPPED UP SOMEWHERE!
THE KIDS ARE SURE PUZZLED! I THINK I'LL KEEP STILL ABOUT MY RADAR SET FOR A WHILE!
WE'VE FINISHED THE DISHES, UNCA' DONALD!
MAY WE GO OVER TO HERBERT'S HOUSE
AND PLAY?
NO! IT'S TIME TO MOW THE LAWN!... AND DON'T TRY ANY TRICKS—I WANT TO TAKE A NAP!
Z Z Z
WE CAN'T KEEP THIS UP!
NO! IT'S TOO MUCH FUN!
UNCA' DONALD IS SLEEPING— LET'S SCRAM!

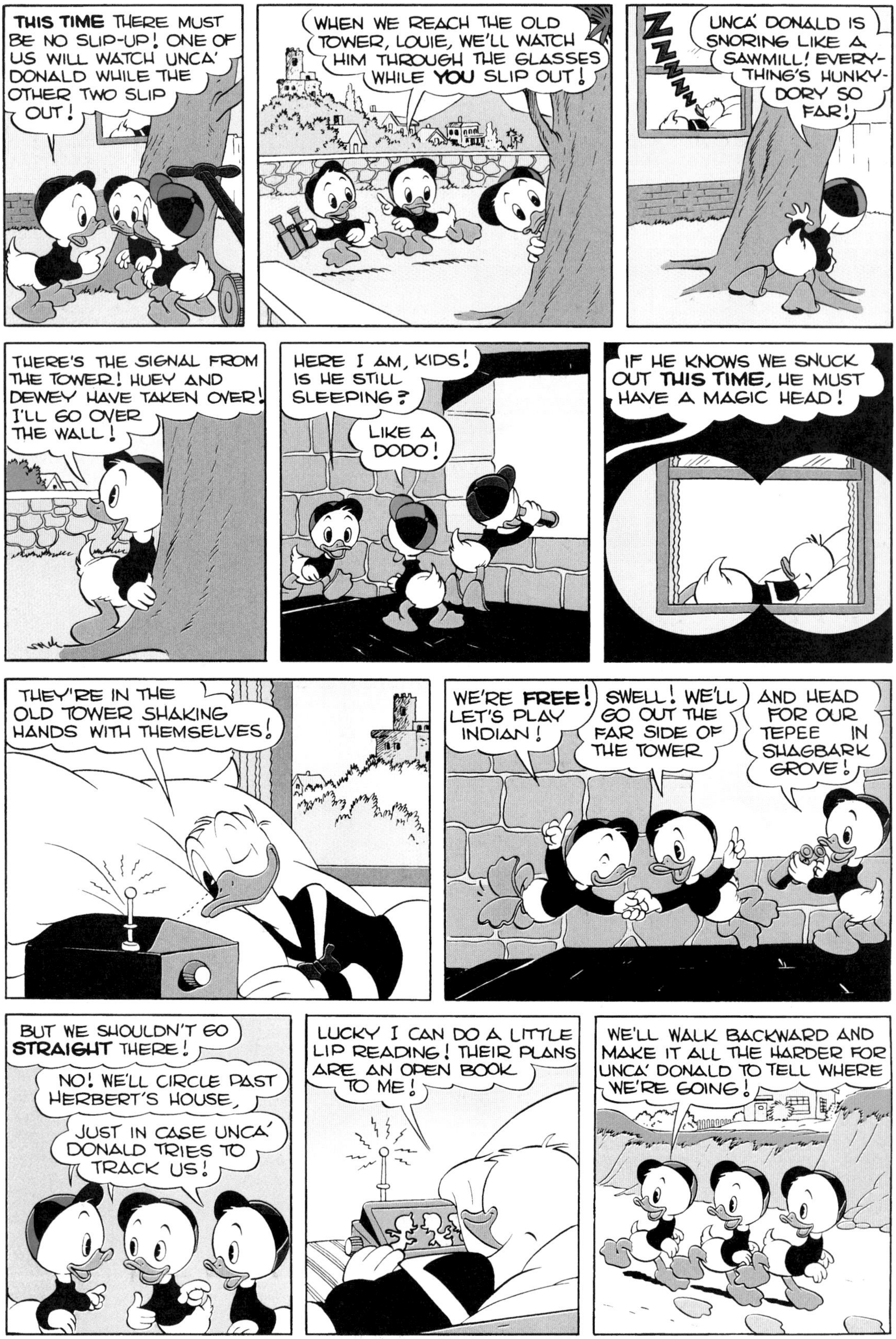
THIS TIME THERE MUST BE NO SLIP-UP! ONE OF US WILL WATCH UNCA' DONALD WHILE THE OTHER TWO SLIP OUT!
WHEN WE REACH THE OLD TOWER, LOUIE, WE'LL WATCH HIM THROUGH THE GLASSES WHILE YOU SLIP OUT!
ZZZZZZ
UNCA' DONALD IS SNORING LIKE A SAWMILL! EVERYTHING'S HUNKY-DORY SO FAR!
THERE'S THE SIGNAL FROM THE TOWER! HUEY AND DEWEY HAVE TAKEN OVER! I'LL GO OVER THE WALL!
HERE I AM, KIDS! IS HE STILL SLEEPING?
LIKE A DODO!
IF HE KNOWS WE SNUCK OUT THIS TIME, HE MUST HAVE A MAGIC HEAD!
THEY'RE IN THE OLD TOWER SHAKING HANDS WITH THEMSELVES!
WE'RE FREE! LET'S PLAY INDIAN!
SWELL! WE'LL GO OUT THE FAR SIDE OF THE TOWER
AND HEAD FOR OUR TEPEE IN SHAGBARK GROVE!
BUT WE SHOULDN'T GO STRAIGHT THERE!
NO! WE'LL CIRCLE PAST HERBERT'S HOUSE,
JUST IN CASE UNCA' DONALD TRIES TO TRACK US!
LUCKY I CAN DO A LITTLE LIP READING! THEIR PLANS ARE AN OPEN BOOK TO ME!
WE'LL WALK BACKWARD AND MAKE IT ALL THE HARDER FOR UNCA' DONALD TO TELL WHERE WE'RE GOING!

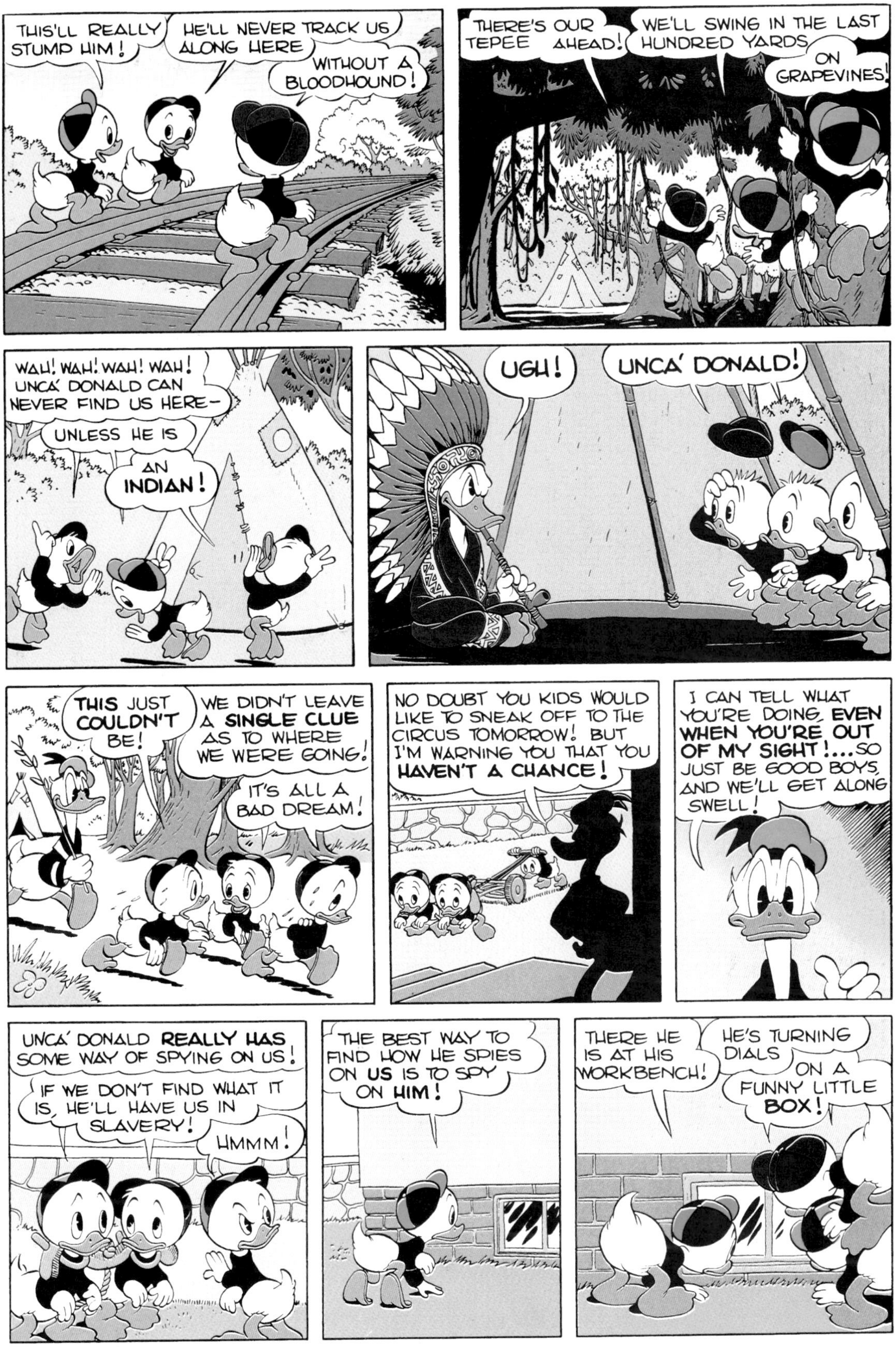
THIS'LL REALLY STUMP HIM!
HE'LL NEVER TRACK US ALONG HERE
WITHOUT A BLOODHOUND!
THERE'S OUR TEPEE AHEAD!
WE'LL SWING IN THE LAST HUNDRED YARDS
ON GRAPEVINES!
WAH! WAH! WAH! WAH! UNCA' DONALD CAN NEVER FIND US HERE—
UNLESS HE IS
AN INDIAN!
UGH!
UNCA' DONALD!
THIS JUST COULDN'T BE!
WE DIDN'T LEAVE A SINGLE CLUE AS TO WHERE WE WERE GOING!
IT'S ALL A BAD DREAM!
NO DOUBT YOU KIDS WOULD LIKE TO SNEAK OFF TO THE CIRCUS TOMORROW! BUT I'M WARNING YOU THAT YOU HAVEN'T A CHANCE!
I CAN TELL WHAT YOU'RE DOING, EVEN WHEN YOU'RE OUT OF MY SIGHT!... SO JUST BE GOOD BOYS, AND WE'LL GET ALONG SWELL!
UNCA' DONALD REALLY HAS SOME WAY OF SPYING ON US!
IF WE DON'T FIND WHAT IT IS, HE'LL HAVE US IN SLAVERY!
HMMM!
THE BEST WAY TO FIND HOW HE SPIES ON US IS TO SPY ON HIM!
THERE HE IS AT HIS WORKBENCH!
HE'S TURNING DIALS
ON A FUNNY LITTLE BOX!

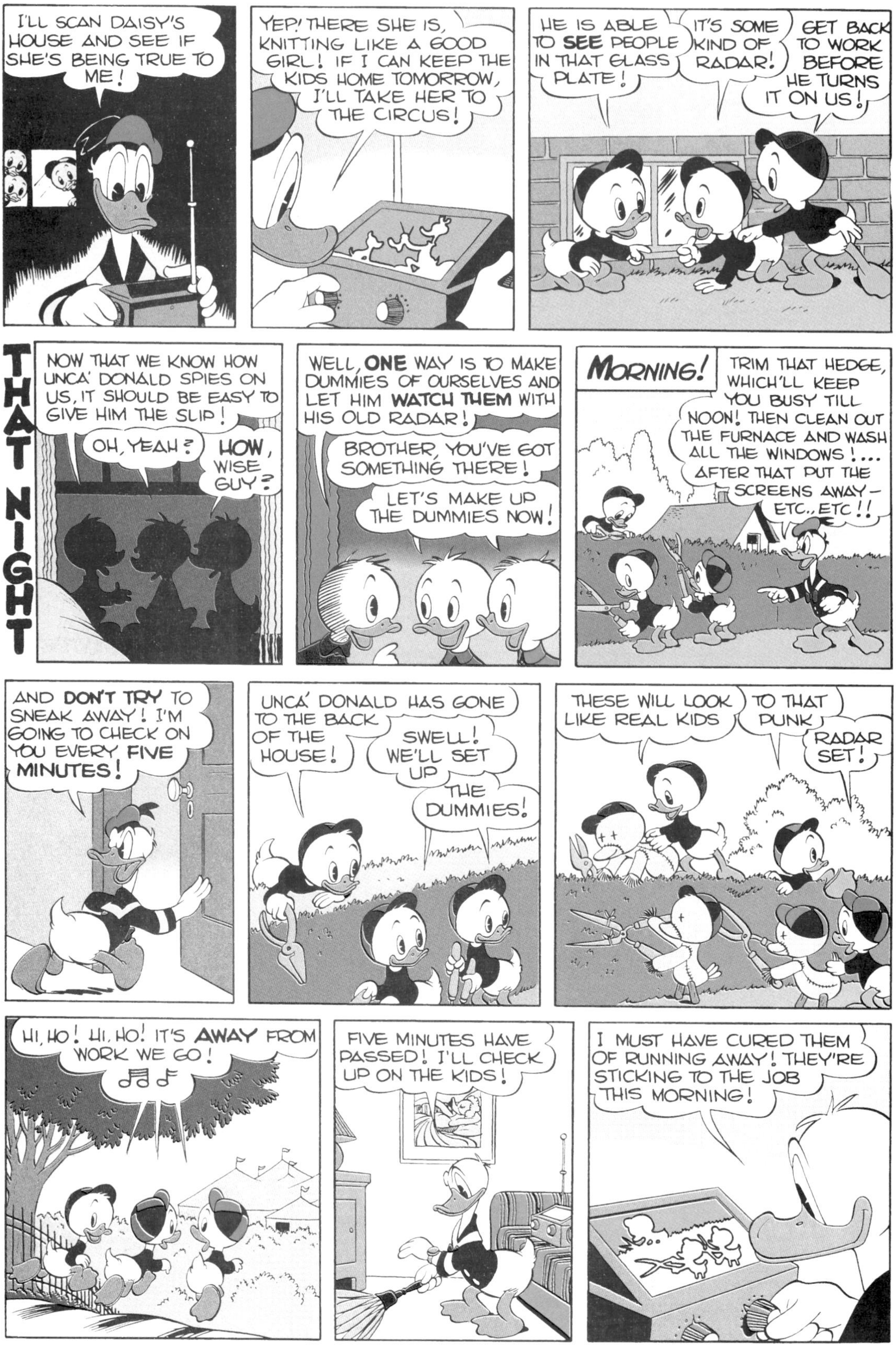
I'LL SCAN DAISY'S HOUSE AND SEE IF SHE'S BEING TRUE TO ME!
YEP! THERE SHE IS, KNITTING LIKE A GOOD GIRL! IF I CAN KEEP THE KIDS HOME TOMORROW, I'LL TAKE HER TO THE CIRCUS!
HE IS ABLE TO SEE PEOPLE IN THAT GLASS PLATE!
IT'S SOME KIND OF RADAR!
GET BACK TO WORK BEFORE HE TURNS IT ON US!
THAT NIGHT
NOW THAT WE KNOW HOW UNCA' DONALD SPIES ON US, IT SHOULD BE EASY TO GIVE HIM THE SLIP!
OH, YEAH?
HOW, WISE GUY?
WELL, ONE WAY IS TO MAKE DUMMIES OF OURSELVES AND LET HIM WATCH THEM WITH HIS OLD RADAR!
BROTHER, YOU'VE GOT SOMETHING THERE!
LET'S MAKE UP THE DUMMIES NOW!
MORNING!
TRIM THAT HEDGE, WHICH'LL KEEP YOU BUSY TILL NOON! THEN CLEAN OUT THE FURNACE AND WASH ALL THE WINDOWS!... AFTER THAT PUT THE SCREENS AWAY– ETC., ETC!!
AND DON'T TRY TO SNEAK AWAY! I'M GOING TO CHECK ON YOU EVERY FIVE MINUTES!
UNCA' DONALD HAS GONE TO THE BACK OF THE HOUSE!
SWELL! WE'LL SET UP
THE DUMMIES!
THESE WILL LOOK LIKE REAL KIDS
TO THAT PUNK
RADAR SET!
HI, HO! HI, HO! IT'S AWAY FROM WORK WE GO!
FIVE MINUTES HAVE PASSED! I'LL CHECK UP ON THE KIDS!
I MUST HAVE CURED THEM OF RUNNING AWAY! THEY'RE STICKING TO THE JOB THIS MORNING!

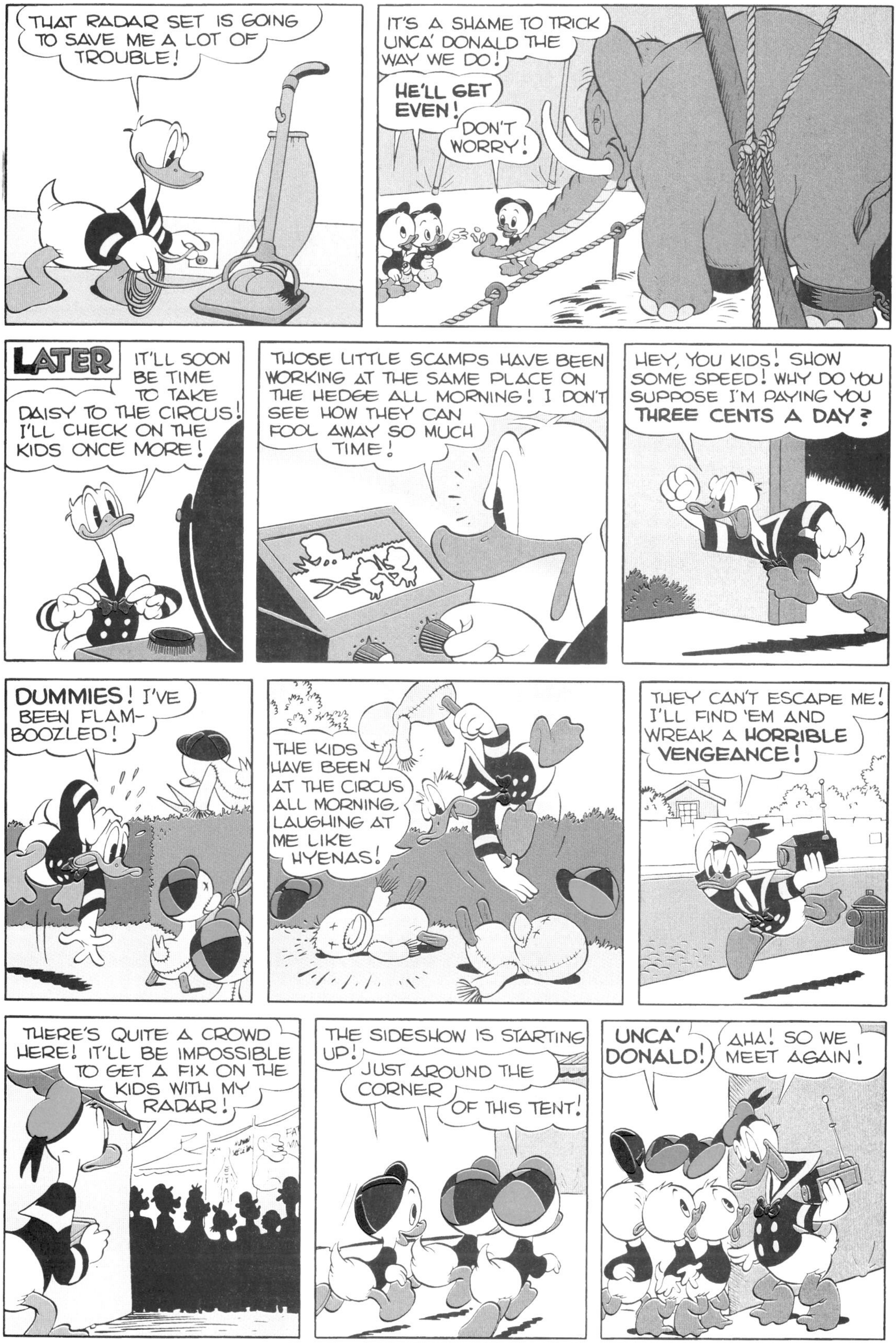
THAT RADAR SET IS GOING TO SAVE ME A LOT OF TROUBLE!
IT'S A SHAME TO TRICK UNCA' DONALD THE WAY WE DO!
HE'LL GET EVEN!
DON'T WORRY!
LATER
IT'LL SOON BE TIME TO TAKE DAISY TO THE CIRCUS! I'LL CHECK ON THE KIDS ONCE MORE!
THOSE LITTLE SCAMPS HAVE BEEN WORKING AT THE SAME PLACE ON THE HEDGE ALL MORNING! I DON'T SEE HOW THEY CAN FOOL AWAY SO MUCH TIME!
HEY, YOU KIDS! SHOW SOME SPEED! WHY DO YOU SUPPOSE I'M PAYING YOU THREE CENTS A DAY?
DUMMIES! I'VE BEEN FLAM-BOOZLED!
THE KIDS HAVE BEEN AT THE CIRCUS ALL MORNING, LAUGHING AT ME LIKE HYENAS!
THEY CAN'T ESCAPE ME! I'LL FIND 'EM AND WREAK A HORRIBLE VENGEANCE!
THERE'S QUITE A CROWD HERE! IT'LL BE IMPOSSIBLE TO GET A FIX ON THE KIDS WITH MY RADAR!
THE SIDESHOW IS STARTING UP!
JUST AROUND THE CORNER
OF THIS TENT!
UNCA' DONALD!
AHA! SO WE MEET AGAIN!

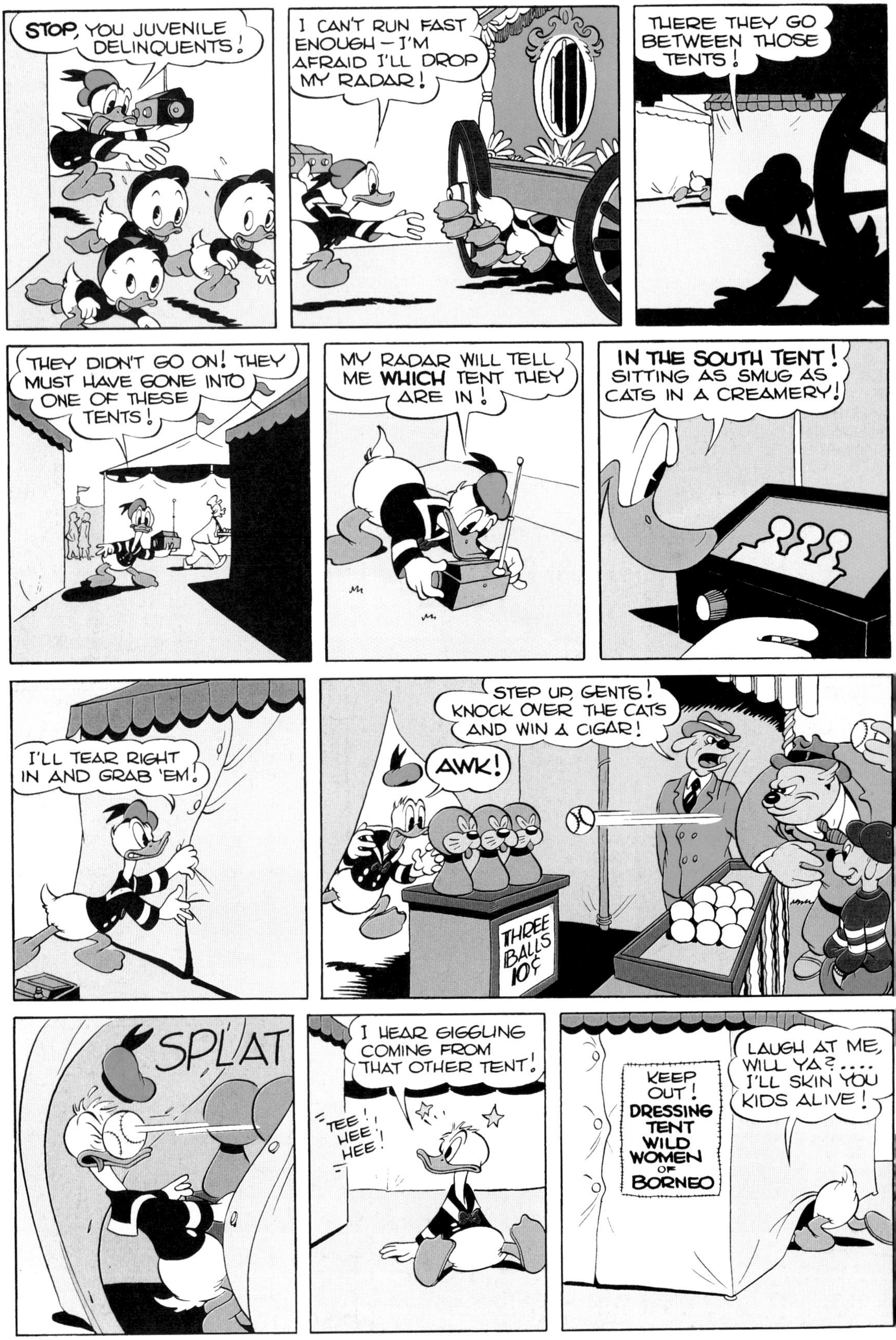
STOP, YOU JUVENILE DELINQUENTS!
I CAN'T RUN FAST ENOUGH — I'M AFRAID I'LL DROP MY RADAR!
THERE THEY GO BETWEEN THOSE TENTS!
THEY DIDN'T GO ON! THEY MUST HAVE GONE INTO ONE OF THESE TENTS!
MY RADAR WILL TELL ME WHICH TENT THEY ARE IN!
IN THE SOUTH TENT! SITTING AS SMUG AS CATS IN A CREAMERY!
I'LL TEAR RIGHT IN AND GRAB 'EM!
STEP UP, GENTS! KNOCK OVER THE CATS AND WIN A CIGAR!
AWK!
THREE BALLS 10¢
SPLAT
I HEAR GIGGLING COMING FROM THAT OTHER TENT!
TEE! HEE! HEE!
KEEP OUT! DRESSING TENT WILD WOMEN OF BORNEO
LAUGH AT ME, WILL YA?.... I'LL SKIN YOU KIDS ALIVE!

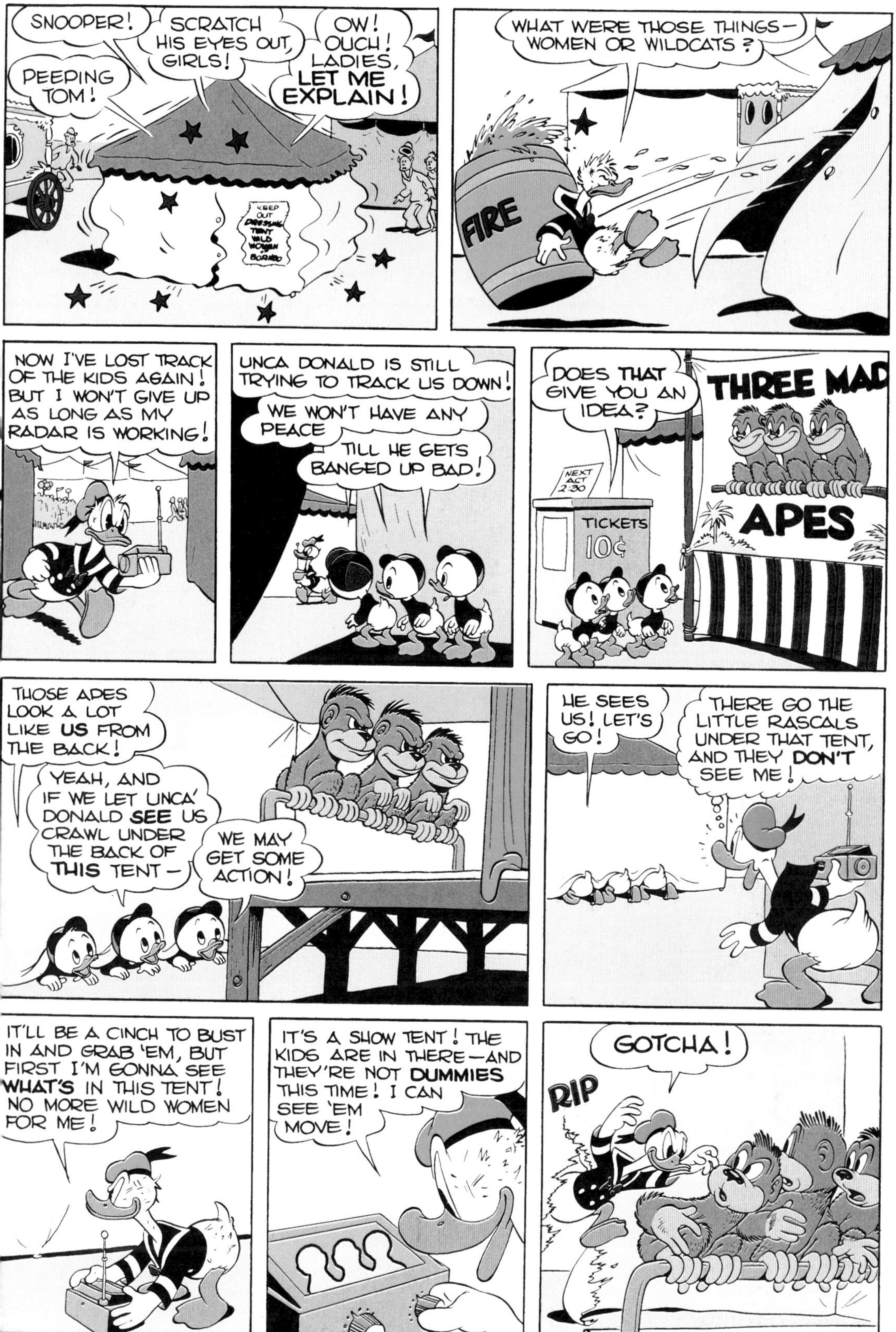
SNOOPER!
PEEPING TOM!
SCRATCH HIS EYES OUT, GIRLS!
OW! OUCH! LADIES, LET ME EXPLAIN!
KEEP OUT DRESSING TENT WILD WOMEN OF BORNEO
WHAT WERE THOSE THINGS— WOMEN OR WILDCATS?
FIRE
NOW I'VE LOST TRACK OF THE KIDS AGAIN! BUT I WON'T GIVE UP AS LONG AS MY RADAR IS WORKING!
UNCA DONALD IS STILL TRYING TO TRACK US DOWN!
WE WON'T HAVE ANY PEACE
TILL HE GETS BANGED UP BAD!
DOES THAT GIVE YOU AN IDEA?
NEXT ACT 2:30
TICKETS 10¢
THREE MAD
APES
THOSE APES LOOK A LOT LIKE US FROM THE BACK!
YEAH, AND IF WE LET UNCA' DONALD SEE US CRAWL UNDER THE BACK OF THIS TENT—
WE MAY GET SOME ACTION!
HE SEES US! LET'S GO!
THERE GO THE LITTLE RASCALS UNDER THAT TENT, AND THEY DON'T SEE ME!
IT'LL BE A CINCH TO BUST IN AND GRAB 'EM, BUT FIRST I'M GONNA SEE WHAT'S IN THIS TENT! NO MORE WILD WOMEN FOR ME!
IT'S A SHOW TENT! THE KIDS ARE IN THERE—AND THEY'RE NOT DUMMIES THIS TIME! I CAN SEE 'EM MOVE!
GOTCHA!
RIP

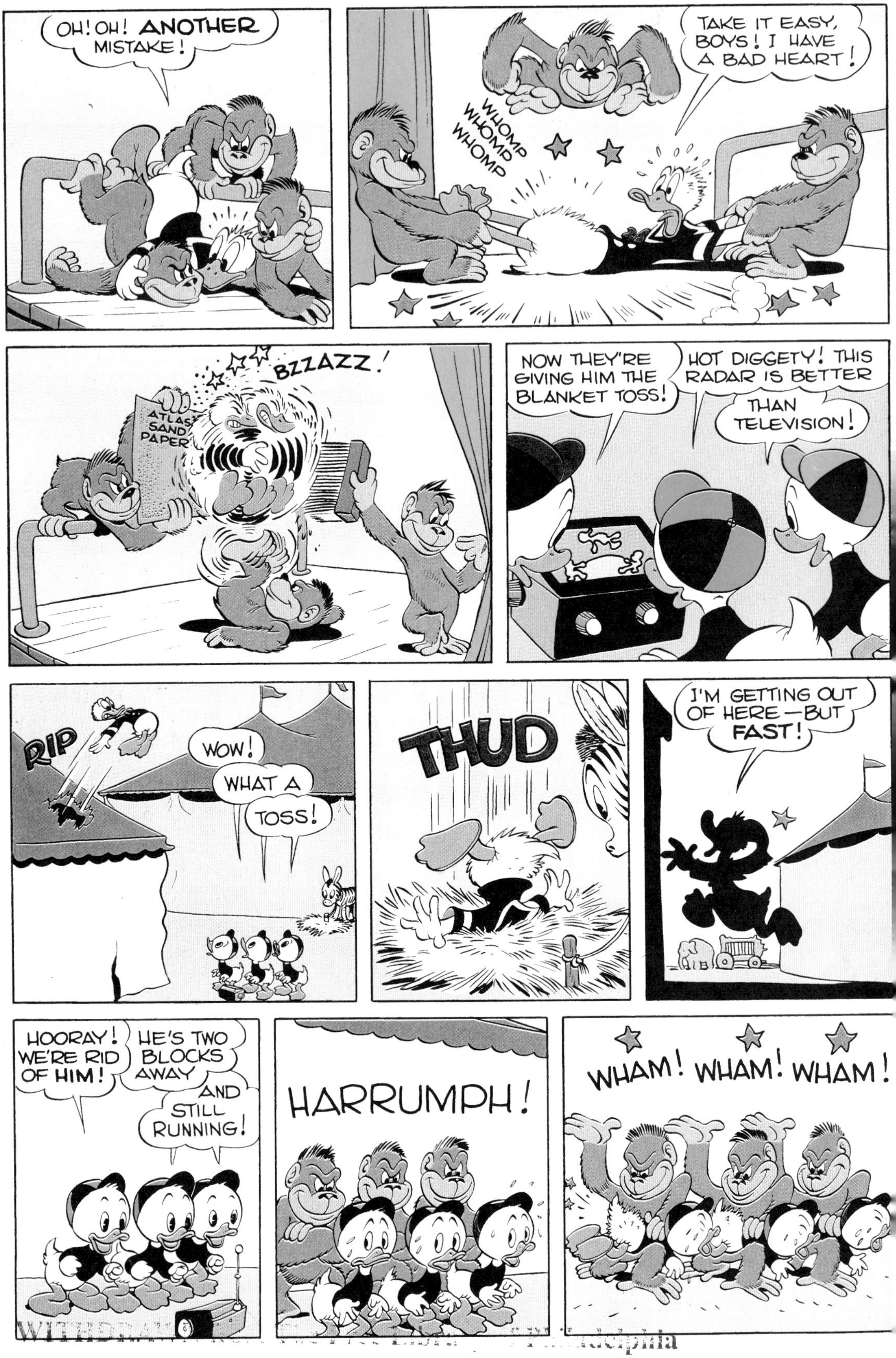
OH! OH! ANOTHER MISTAKE!
TAKE IT EASY, BOYS! I HAVE A BAD HEART!
WHOMP WHOMP WHOMP
BZZAZZ!
ATLAS SAND PAPER
NOW THEY'RE GIVING HIM THE BLANKET TOSS!
HOT DIGGETY! THIS RADAR IS BETTER
THAN TELEVISION!
RIP
WOW!
WHAT A
TOSS!
THUD
I'M GETTING OUT OF HERE—BUT FAST!
HOORAY! WE'RE RID OF HIM!
HE'S TWO BLOCKS AWAY
AND STILL RUNNING!
HARRUMPH!
WHAM! WHAM! WHAM!